THIS BOOK
WILL GET
YOU LAID

THIS BOOK WILL GET YOU LAID

E. Dickens

Michael O'Mara Books Limited

First published in 2006 by
Michael O'Mara Books Limited
9 Lion Yard
Tremadoc Road
London SW4 7NQ

A CIP catalogue record for this book is available from the British Library.

ISBN (10 digit): 1-84317-198-8
ISBN (13 digit): 978-1-84317-198-0

1 3 5 7 9 10 8 6 4 2

Designed by www.burville-riley.com

Printed and bound in Great Britain by Cox & Wyman, Reading, Berks

www.mombooks.com

Contents

Acknowledgements   7

Introduction   9

Twenty Questions – Who Are You?   13

Hey, Good Lookin'   27

Choosing Your Hunting Ground: Part One   41

Hunting, Gathering and Getting Laid   53

Choosing Your Hunting Ground: Part Two   63

Moving in for the Kill   81

Playing with Your Prey   109

Consuming Your Prey   131

Appendix: After the Event   151

Acknowledgements

For cake and case studies, my thanks to Cath, Elizabeth and Helen. Thanks also to Cailey and Giggsy. As ever, I am indebted to Pels and Kate – and to Screenie, although she doesn't know it – Jodders. Igor, Mark and Beck, Uncle Bri, Michele and Neek – thanks guys. Thanks also to Lindsay Davies and Kate Gribble, of course. And sorry to anyone I've forgotten – I plead the sleep deprivation a brand new baby brings.

Introduction

It's always hunting season. A simple fact often overlooked by men is that everybody wants to be wanted and everybody wants to pull. If it's a game, it's one with goalposts a world's width apart. Open your mind to this and the fact that opportunities are everywhere, and you're most of the way there. But do so lightly, not as though your life depends on it. Yes, you want to get laid, but desperation is off-putting. Be cool, and you're much more likely to get coital.

You may have heard of the bestselling 2005 book *The Game*, by Neil Strauss, which tells of the exploits of a handful of average men who hone their pick-up skills to the extent that they can pull any woman they choose. The book has been a runaway success, with many average men hoping to replicate the experiences it describes. But there's a problem: *The Game* falls down because the pick-up artist out on the town is not who you really are. The sad fact is that it's an act, whether or not your audience falls for the showman and chooses to go home with him. Imagine being 'on' whenever you're out. That's not a game, it's a job. It's for the geeky guy who couldn't get a date, is scarred by the fact and will sacrifice everything to compensate for it.

Women like honesty, confidence and friendliness. The cool girls, the ones you want to attract, will see through professional pick-up artists before they even open their mouths. So what's a guy to do? Imagine finding the sexiest, most charming you imaginable and letting him loose in public places. That's what *This Book Will Get You*

Laid will help you to do. Show someone that they're a challenge you're capable of rising to and they'll be yours. A woman is not a victim. She can always turn you down. Make it more fun for her not to.

There's a certain type of man who is often to be found whinging on about how women hold all the cards these days and are all ball-breakers, leaving men without a discernible role. Diddums. What should he do? Belt up. I don't think he'd have pulled in any century. We women are as ripe for seduction as we've always been. You just have to be good enough at it.

Which is where this book comes in. *This Book Will Get You Laid* is an advice book with a difference. For I am a spy in the house of lust and I've come to tell you everything, giving you an 'access-all-areas' pass into the minds of the women you've got in your sights. Within these pages you will gain exclusive insights into how we think, which men we'll sleep with, which we won't and sure-fire ways to make yourself a sexual success.

Other books tie themselves in knots about whether or not to use chat-up lines. I say it doesn't matter as long as a smile is the result. They can work. When a fireman, asked whether he'd met me before, said, 'No, I'd have remembered,' I wasn't thinking about how many women he'd said it to before. Ditto the guy who told me, 'This body should be dressed in nothing but Gucci and Prada.'

Chat-up lines are only the start of it, however. Whether you need a bit of guidance on meeting the ladies or on closing the deal, you'll learn all the manoeuvres necessary for getting from 'hello' to the bedroom – plus fail-safe ways of flirting a woman into the sack. Pinpoint the secret seduction techniques that will have her eating out of your hand. And it doesn't stop there. Discover how to drive your woman wild in bed and become a real red-hot lover with a

Pulling Your Partner

Of course, for some of you the actual hunting down and capturing of the prey may already have been achieved. You may already have a partner. But those in relationships are *supposed* to be getting an average of three times as much sex as single people. Do you suspect you're not? The trick is to keep capturing her, over and over again. In other words, you must keep her feeling like she's being seduced. Throughout the book, you will find a number of 'Pulling Your Partner' sections, which are designed to give you some ideas about how.

reputation to rival Casanova's. With checklists, tips, guides and revelations, this book is your one-way ticket to no-strings sexual nirvana.

So come with me, and remember – you're not nervous, you're excited ...

1
Twenty Questions – Who Are You?

So here you are, reasonably good-looking, pretty intelligent, sound of body, mind and spirit. Yet the last time a woman voluntarily went back to your flat was when you were interviewing for a new cleaner. What's the problem? You need a long, hard ... look at yourself. Yes, I know quizzes are a bit girly, but go with me on this. Have a look at the questions below. Don't take too long thinking about your replies – just go with the first one that feels right. You'll be on the road to recovery in no time.

1 Okay, first things first. How would others describe your driving?
   a) Ballsy. Fun. Never a dull moment.
   b) Functional – gets you from A to B safely.
   c) I don't drive.
   d) Fast and furious. Most friends won't accompany me any more.
   e) I tend to get lifts, but if I drive I'm pretty good.

2 What about your table manners?
   a) Always ravenous; always leave a clean plate.
   b) I don't expect anyone would notice them.
   c) Impeccable.
   d) Who cares?
   e) Passable, I expect.

3 What's your all-time favourite television show?
a) *Pimp My Ride.*
b) *ER.*
c) Anything about the Second World War.
d) *The Simpsons*, though more of a gamer myself.
e) *Seinfeld.*

4 How about movie?
a) *Terminator 2.*
b) *Dirty Dancing.*
c) *Trop Belle Pour Toi.*
d) *The Matrix.*
e) *Magnolia.*

5 Computer game?
a) *Grand Theft Auto: San Andreas.*
b) *SimCity.*
c) Eh?
d) *Burnout Revenge.*
e) *Championship Manager.*

6 What are your feelings about pornography?
a) Yes please, at every opportunity.
b) If she introduced it, perhaps.
c) I don't believe in it. It exploits women. Unless it didn't, in which case I might find it arousing ...
d) Do people get off without porn on the TV in the background?
e) I partake every now and again. Never really thought about using it with a partner.

7 Who's your ideal woman?
   a) Kelly Brook.
   b) Katie Holmes.
   c) Camille Paglia.
   d) A female.
   e) Reese Witherspoon.

8 What's your favourite animal?
   a) Tiger.
   b) Cat.
   c) Dolphin.
   d) Dog.
   e) White rabbit.

9 Which aroma does it for you?
   a) Women.
   b) Chanel No. 5.
   c) Lavender oil.
   d) Car grease.
   e) Vanilla.

10 What's your favourite colour?
   a) Purple – for passion.
   b) White – all colours are absorbed into it.
   c) Burnt sienna – makes me think of Tuscany in late summer.
   d) British racing green.
   e) Blue – for the sea and the sky.

11 Okay, let's go back to your school days ...

a) Best years of my life. If only it were still that simple ...

b) A confusing time. Howard always got the girls and all I got were good marks.

c) Good idea. That way we can trace the root cause of the problem, right?

d) What's the point of that? I thought we were trying to get laid now. Let's crack on.

e) Yeah, they were okay, I guess. Wasn't too fussed about them either way.

12 How were things with the girls in those days? Lots of girlfriends or a bit of a loser?

a) I could pretty much take my pick.

b) Not much action. One or two girlfriends but they didn't go anywhere much.

c) I was a bit immature for all that. Kept my head down, on the whole.

d) A bit of smooching at the disco, a bit of a grope, then she was gone.

e) Yeah, there were girls, you know the kind of thing. Kids' stuff, really. Didn't get too involved.

13 When did you lose your virginity?

a) Twelve – I held out as long as I could.

b) Seventeen. We were in love. It was the right time.

c) Give me a chance.

d) Fourteen – we were drunk. It was the first and last time we met.

e) Sixteen. I don't recall who was first. They were all great girls, though.

16

14 By some miracle, you've got her back to your place. Which CD do you put on?

a) Something ambient and sexy.

b) I ask her what she'd like to hear.

c) Italian opera.

d) There's no need for seduction music – we'll be making sweet music of our own in no time.

e) Every girl's different – I'd browse through my entire collection before making a decision.

15 Well, it's worked. You've been kissing passionately on the sofa for five minutes. What's your next move?

a) It's got to be a little stroking, followed by the one-handed bra release.

b) Maybe I'd offer her a massage.

c) She'd show me what she wanted.

d) I'd take her into the bedroom.

e) I'd see how the mood took me. Chemistry would carry us through ...

16 Ah. That wasn't so successful. She's saying, 'I can't.' She's drawing away from you. She's finding her jacket and getting ready to go. What are you going to do? Quick!

a) Eh? What's going on? We were getting on so well! You're making a mistake ...

b) I think she's right. We've only just met. It was moving too fast. I'll call her a cab.

c) I knew it was too good to be true. Should I have played her the Wagner instead?

d) You run along, darling. Your loss.

e) Just one of those things. There'll be others.

17 What happens after sex at your place?
   a) A smoke and a spot of MTV usually.
   b) A long, meaningful conversation.
   c) Perhaps an after-play massage and a light salad.
   d) Sleep or food. With or without the girl.
   e) There's usually been a long build-up to it, so we just enjoy each other.

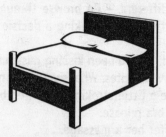

18 Why did your last relationship end?
   a) I couldn't keep it in my pants.
   b) We stopped fancying each other.
   c) It was complicated – a mixture of reasons.
   d) She left me for a teacher.
   e) She wanted more than I could give.

19 What would your most recent ex – or current partner – say about your attitude towards women and sex?
   a) That I'm obsessed – but I'm a man, aren't I? What did she expect?
   b) That she was too pushy – or possibly that I'm frightened of them and it.
   c) That I appreciate them for the wonderful creatures they are.
   d) That I'm up for it.
   e) That it's pretty good; I'm definitely not a misogynist, but I'm not a feminist either.

20 What are your relationships with your exes like?

    a) I still acknowledge them in the street. Most I sleep with a couple of times a year.

    b) Good, all of them. In fact, I devote a lot of time to wondering whether I should still be with each of them in turn.

    c) I'm keen, having made that emotional investment, but they don't always return my calls.

    d) No relationships with exes. That's what 'ex' means.

    e) Pretty good on the whole. Perhaps some even carry a torch for me.

Conclusion

Now add up your total number of a)s, b)s, c)s, d)s and e)s to find out who you are.

Mostly a)s – Alpha Male

You think you're the life and soul of the party. You wear those jeans with the faded patches under the pockets: the problem is, spiritually if not sartorially you're stuck in the 1950s. Women are either virgins or whores to you – and as far as you're concerned, you're a bit of a catch whoever they are.

It's not your fault, it's your parents'. They gave you the idea that you were entitled to every happiness without putting in any effort – and that there would always be a woman around to take care of the boring shit. To your surprise, it's not quite as simple as that in the real world.

You have enough success with women to keep your high opinion of yourself pretty high. The good news with you is that you at least grab life by the bollocks, which is more than 90 per cent of the world's population does. This is the single most attractive thing in a person and all sorts of people will forgive all sorts of crassness to be around it.

The problems? You don't often listen. Your intended prey may be smiling sweetly and nodding while you talk at her, but in her head, when she contemplates going home with you, images of mundane humping and waiting for you to climax persist. Bear this in mind when you're wondering why you don't have the roaring success with women that one with your charisma deserves. You think that if you look good, they'll come running and you won't have to do a thing. On the contrary, all of the most successful pick-up artists put effort in – they just disguise it well.

For the future, work on listening to people. Have a conversation, rather than giving another lecture on how great you are. Try not to be slick, or too much of a poseur – it's suspicious and off-putting. Instead, dig deep and find a bit of sensitivity. That, combined with your good looks and natural confidence, will reap big rewards.

Mostly b)s – The Eternal Best Friend

You've got more attractive female friends than anyone you know and you fancy all of them a bit. So why aren't you getting laid more often? Your male friends say girls think you're either gay or asexual. The girls who don't share their view think they're too dirty for you and you'll die of shock if you go to bed together.

I think your main problem is that you're a coward: you're always hedging your bets. You don't have to be a red-blooded stud to be non-committal. You can just fail to jump feet first into anything – including sex.

Perhaps you've convinced yourself that you're a good guy who can't seem to find the right girl. That's the easy way out. You give mixed messages to your girlfriends –

perhaps they're your One, it's just that the two of you haven't realized it yet – keeping them all within reach. (You can tell if you're one of these chaps by the fact that your girlfriends are never introduced to one another, and by the spitting rage you find yourself flying into whenever one of them gets fed up and gets a partner or, worse, gets married or has a baby.) In your mind you have a kind of modern-day harem of choices – it's just that its members don't know they're in it.

The good news is that you're one of the good guys. At heart you are worried about hurting someone's feelings. You're not sure how you feel about her, so you don't want to act on any initial attraction, just in case it fails to fulfil its potential. But be aware, she may not care. She may not dream of babies and houses in the country when she thinks of you. She may just be wondering why all this repressed sexual energy has been flying around the two of you all these years, and want to have a wild session to get it out of both your systems.

Ask yourself what you really want. Have you got an ideal in your head that you can't let go of? Is it your mother; your ex; a French actress? If so, take heed: *she doesn't exist*. That's what an ideal is, and you're destined to be a lonely man if you don't cotton on to that fact.

If you want to get laid more, you need to be more committed to being alive. I think you're a charismatic man or you wouldn't have so many female friends, but they're starting to spot that you offer the bare minimum to keep the relationship going. You're going to have to give more of yourself. Take the plunge, and soak up some success.

Mostly c)s – Mediocre New Man

You've got all the right gear; you're solvent; you pride yourself on being a gentleman. What's the problem? You're boring, friend. You've probably got a degree but nothing else about you. You're over-prepared, yet completely ill-equipped. Like Best Mate above, you don't give enough of yourself to be the kind of man girls want to take home and be ravished by.

Has no one told you that girls don't give a toss for shiny new technical things? Stop showing her your new iPod and start showing her a good time. That you know a bit about rap doesn't make you an angry young rebel who plays by his own rules, it makes you a trainspotter who's turned his attention to rap produced by angry young rebels ...

You're a geek and deep down you know you are. But learn that this is cool. Forgive yourself. Some of the most successful pick-up artists in the world came to it late in life. And there's a geek who can't pull in all of us. We just bury him alive daily. You need to distinguish yourself from the crowd. Make a feature of your geekiness. Use that sense of humour you built up against bullies to seduce her. Think Woody Allen. Present a challenge. Decide you're a prize to be won. This is your time now. Dazzle her mind. Show her what you learned while she was kissing the leader of the pack – though perhaps not the stuff about refraction and quadratic equations.

And at the same time, learn that it's okay to be sexual, whoever you are. Show her your inner animal – but easy, tiger: it might come as something of a surprise after all those years of early nights and heading home alone.

Mostly d)s – The Fool Who Rushes In

If a job's worth doing, it's worth doing in a half-arsed, rushed way, right? And it's just the same with women, right? There isn't time to mess around investing in something that's unlikely to pay you dividends, is there? Not in any context?

You are, of course, sabotaging your chances with women with this carefree, careless attitude, and you must be aware of this on some level. Everybody knows that 'care' and 'attention' are the bywords for females, don't they? I think you do know that, but you've long ago given up on perfection and are settling for nothing at all instead. In fact, I think you're something of a disappointed romantic.

Either that, or you're not very bright. Are you a victim of your throwaway culture, perhaps? Are you something of a Starbucks shag? Quick, everywhere all at once, low quality, predictable, perfectly disposable? You act like you don't think about anything much. Like life throws itself at you and you have a full-time job fending it off. There is a life to be led like this, of course, but unfortunately for you, my friend, it is at odds with seducing all but the drunkest, most desperate of women.

Ask yourself what you're rushing towards. This is all there is. Nothing better is on its way. There's a cartoon which runs through the character's collection of underpants, day by day, working up to the Sunday 'special pair' of underpants. The character says with unforgettable poignancy, 'One day, every day will be a special-pants day.' Not so. The same applies to that part in the movie *Sideways* (2004), where the female character says that he should not be waiting for the right occasion to drink the 1961 wine because drinking the 1961 wine *is* the occasion. If you grasp this, then you can have any woman you choose.

You're not just an animal. You need to bother refining yourself – it's fun, I promise. Learn to slow down and take your time over making a proper meal. Let your appearance cross your mind before you go out. Just for once, go clothes shopping with a female friend. Value your own life more. Take control of it. Savour it. It'll pay off, mark my words.

Mostly e)s – Mr 'Time Is On My Side'

Firstly, no it's not. You don't have all the time in the world to make your move, my friend. You have an optimum number of meetings to stake your claim, after which she'll assume you're not interested and find someone else. If there is no statement of intent – however subtle – by the second date, and if she has any self-respect, she'll start looking for her bedfellows elsewhere. In fact, if she has any self-respect she'll be looking for them even as she spends time with you.

This is a metropolitan disease. It's to do with risk aversion. But search your relationship memory bank and you'll find that 'spark' and 'massive delay' do not often appear in the same file. Deferred gratification is one thing; but you have to know there's potential gratification to be deferred first. You're probably protecting your great single life by being so passive, but is it really that great? Haven't you got the hang of getting drunk in bars with your mates and going home alone by now?

Because you're essentially a liberal man, you think that women are much like men – but 'equal' does not mean the same. There are fundamental differences in the minds of the two sexes. Difference is sexy – exotic. If you can make a woman feel like she's different from you and endlessly fascinating – even if she isn't – you're away.

The truth is, you think that you have an idea about how people tick and that you're a little superior to the conceited alpha male and his ilk, but at least he's got some get-up-and-go. He's sucking the marrow out of life. He has grasped the idea that we live once. And it probably gets him laid more often than you.

So don't take your time. Don't weigh up every girl to see if she's worth bothering to get to know. By the time you've made your calculations, she'll have moved on. Seize the day. Don't wait six months to call her: call her this week. The quicker you move, the quicker you'll get laid – you see, there is something in it for you. Go for it.

11
Hey, Good Lookin'

First things first. No self-respecting girl is going to go with you if you smell like a sewer and have only the vaguest notion of how you look. Don't get me wrong: looks aren't everything. You don't even have to have good fashion sense in order to get laid. But there are some things that'll help your cause. This chapter doesn't focus on chat-up lines or where to find those lovely ladies you're going to lay – we're going back to basics instead. First impressions count for a lot. So let's make sure she's interested in you before you even open your mouth.

Perhaps you're one of those men who believe it's time men began strutting their stuff like the peacocks they're really meant to be? Well, fair enough, but you need to be sure that your target market agrees with you, and doesn't just think you're a bit vain after all that effort. I'm all for the loud Hawaiian shirt or a well-cut suit in a bright colour, but anything that screams 'Look at me!' too loudly will make me look away.

Don't be fetid, but don't get too hung up on grooming. Less is more. Whatever you do, don't groom too rigorously, especially the hair – we'll worry about breaking you in bed if your quiff is stiffer than your cock. Never look prissy or fussy. When a friend's ex insisted on the milk going in before the tea bag, she observed inwardly: 'I can't believe I ever slept with you.'

Take a bit of time with your appearance, but try to ensure that it looks like you didn't and you're just a cool guy who can't help looking good. (NB: In appearance, as in every other respect, you have to be a very cool guy indeed to genuinely not be arsed and still get laid.) Some lads tend towards trying too hard and it shows. 'On the pull' scream your carefully-chosen, ironed T-shirt and fashionable low-slung jeans. 'Keep away' thinks any girl who wants to be treated as an individual rather than an anonymous target.

Everybody – keep it simple. You may once have pulled when you were wearing your best gear and you spent ages thinking about it, but the law of averages dictates that this was always going to happen sooner or later. Remember, it wasn't just your outfit that got you action – it was you. Don't make the mistake of thinking fashion is the be-all and end-all when it comes to getting laid. If it hasn't happened already, one of these days, no matter how groomed you are or which of your lucky pulling shirts you have on, your target is going to be snatched from under your nose – by a scruffier, uglier guy with a more assured way about him and a better line than you. 'How could this happen?' you wonder. Well, think about it. If you're more concerned with your Calvin Klein jeans than our conversation, I for one am not going to be keen to achieve a rapport with you. On the other hand, a guy who's attentive, cracks a few jokes, takes an interest in what I have to say and has a genuine, relaxed air about him – well, he's in with a chance, no matter how he's dressed. Above all, remember that physical attractiveness is subjective, but nobody is immune to energy's glamour. Go out to give someone that sudden spark, that unexpected reminder they're alive and you'll have lift-off. I promise.

Grooming and Preparation

Let's start at the beginning. Keep yourself clean and your chances of getting down and dirty are hugely increased. Yes, *some* girls will go for that manly, sweaty look: the mechanic fiddling away beneath a car, grease and oil working into his skin; the footballer triumphant from his latest victory, wet with sweat after ninety minutes on the pitch. But this is the stuff of fantasy, not of fact. A girl actually confronted with your stinky armpit is unlikely to rejoice at the unadulterated masculinity emanating from you – she'll just think you're a pig. While we've occasionally fallen for it in *context* – a generally filthy man being no go, one with reason to be so having slightly more going for him – as a rule we like our men clean and pristine.

So:

- **Take regular showers** (if I'm preaching to the choir, thank the Lord).
- **Keep your hands, especially, super clean.** If all goes well, you'll be laying these on her later – and you don't want her to call a halt to proceedings simply because she can't bear your filthy mitts anywhere near her soft, smooth skin. While we're about it, I hope you always wash your hands after you've been to the lav? I'm not trying to sound like a nursery-school teacher, but believe me, women notice if you haven't – just do it, particularly if you're sharing food together directly afterwards.
- **Take action against weird hairs.** There comes a time in every man's life when weird little hairs start turning up in eyebrows, nostrils and ears. Their sole purpose is to perplex you. Two words you never thought would glide into your orbit: Remington trimmer.

- **Inspect your fingernails.** Keep 'em trimmed short, and scrub beneath them. It is worth investing in a pair of nail scissors rather than biting them down. Think it through: once you're working your way through the 'bases' as planned, those nails (namely, the fingers attached to them) are going to come into contact with something oh so sensitive. It'll be 'Sayonara, sailor' if you hurt her with your unchecked talons.
- **Smell your feet.** Don't make the same mistake as Simon (see the Case Study below). If they stink, take action. See your chemist. Spray some deodorant. As a last resort, keep your shoes on at all times.

Case Study: Simon

'I met someone at a bar once and the chemistry was unbelievable. We went back to my place – which was on the other side of the city from hers – because I had to get up early for a meeting in the morning. She generously paid for the cab back to my house, as I didn't have any cash on me. It cost forty or fifty pounds. I thought I was in there. Then we got inside and I took my trainers off, and you know what? She called a cab straight away and doubled the amount she'd spent by getting the driver to take her all the way back home. Her parting shot was, "I won't sleep with someone with smelly feet." Gutted.'

So you're showered, scrubbed and smelling sweet. What next? The furry stuff – no, don't get ahead of yourself: *your* furry stuff (facial – before you start panicking).

Facial Hair

Opinion has shifted over the past few years about this and as an out-and-out beardiephile I applaud this shift. Beard doesn't have to mean old-school IT geek or academic – although goatee always did and still does mean: 'I might fancy myself a film director, but I'll only ever direct a pop video for a band you've never heard of.'

If you can grow a proper beard – unlike, say, the artist formerly known as Prince – then it's okay to let it get a little beyond the stubble stage, as long as you prune a bit so that wayward hairs don't poke out in every direction. Avoid bushy – she may be interested in your left-wing political ideology or your psychoanalytical theories, but you ain't gonna get laid.

On the subject of 'designer stubble', it's a no for me. It looks great on Hollywood stars and male models, but the practical experience is somewhat disappointing – not to mention painful. It gives you a 'rough-and-ready' look, right? Well, the 'rough' is about right ... which makes us *so* not ready. All those masculine prickles that you enjoy feeling as you run your hand manfully across your cheek? They give us stubble rash. Above *and* below. Ouch.

Hairstyles

Never ponytails, say my team of researchers, and only very styled and 'metrosexual' if you're fourteen or under. Like trousers belted below your bum, if you've moved on from having a skateboard, it's not appropriate. And guys, do move on from having a skateboard or a tiny BMX bike. Don't end up being the guy at work with the secret solitary skateboarding habit – seriously, it won't help you get laid.

Going Grey

Not a problem for us. Honestly. We dig the older, sophisticated look. It makes us feel sophisticated, which makes us like you even more.

Baldness

Depends how you do it is the general consensus. If you're going bald and you shave it off totally, then that's all right. But a little bit of hair in tufts is not an option. You look like 1980s salesmen. Similarly, the combover should be avoided at all costs. Retaining a few long, lone strands of hair does not dupe us into thinking you've got a full head of luscious locks: you just look a bit sad.

Mullet

Forget those eighties footballers, who at the time were the coolest creatures on the planet (to you). Five words on this subject: never in a million years.

On the Catwalk

Right, let's get you dressed. You may think your best chance of pulling a girl is if she sees you in all your glory, ding-dong swinging irresistibly between your hairy thighs, but most girls prefer some gift-wrapping. We'll start at the very beginning: underwear.

The Semiotics of Smalls

You might think you're saying a thousand sexy things with your underpants – but you could be neatly dismissing her with a single statement. If you're wearing briefs, you're saying you're gay, or possibly, 'I'm gay and I don't know it.' If you're wearing novelty pants, you're saying, 'Come back in a few years when I might not be a virgin any more.'

Beyond this, stretchy shorts or boxers from Calvin Klein or Cally Clyde off the market, it's all the same to us. And even if it's not, it's not a deal breaker.

Perhaps it should go without saying that, whatever it is, underwear should be clean. But personal experience tells another story. Please not shorts with the rumpled look of having been worn several days in a row. Or a worse look altogether.

A note about going commando: not as sexy a concept for a woman of a man than vice versa. To us it says, 'Can't be arsed to wash my smalls'/'Haven't got any smalls'. When might this be okay? Nope, can't think of a single occasion.

UNDERWEAR AS OUTERWEAR

Until recently, this was a confusing trend particularly prevalent in young women. 'Is that bra supposed to be there? Should I let her know?' The closest men get to this is being seen in a vest – but make sure you have the body of a young Brando first, or you'll look like pigeon-chested trailer trash.

Men and women both wore their underpants poking out above their trousers up until a few years ago. The legacy of this is jeans belted under the arse leaving the arse/underwear revealed in its entirety. One of those paradoxes that will make your head hurt if you let it. Defying gravity in such a way can only be achieved using the engineering skills of a genius; but could only ever be worn by someone one cable short of a fully functioning suspension bridge.

If you're ever in doubt about what to wear, ask a female friend for advice. If you don't have any or simply can't be

WHY, OH WHY?

- Suit and a baseball cap
- Baseball caps at all in the twenty-first century, unless you're playing baseball
- Jeans and a tie
- Shorts and pulled-up short socks
- Socks and sandals
- Gold jewellery
- Dressing like a teenager when you're thirty-plus
- Dressing like a thirty-year-old when you're a teenager

bothered, go shopping in a store that suits your tastes and personality. Most of the clothes in that one shop can be mixed and matched together, so just buy a shedload of some vaguely coordinating garments and you're away.

You'll probably have a loose idea of what you like and what looks good on you – whether you're a T-shirt or shirt man, whether suits suit you or make you look a dick. As a general rule, wear what you feel comfortable in. This doesn't mean your dog-eared dressing gown and day-old boxers.

Colour on Men

In 2004, US business image consultants decreed that it was okay for men to wear colour – in particular to the office.

On dress-down Fridays, they said it was time to ditch the chinos and polo shirt in favour of pastel trousers and a high-contrast shirt. Well, up to you, guys, but I'm not sure the look would do it for me. They also advise against shorts and sandals at work, but frankly I'd hesitate to take their advice after the pastels suggestion. Surely they're having a laugh at your expense?

Most women would agree that a little colour does no harm, however, and most importantly it sets you apart from the crowd, which is what you need to get laid. So give it a go – if possible getting the opinion of a stylish woman before you go out in public.

Whatever you do, don't go mad. Everything in moderation. *Never* dress head-to-toe in the same colour.

SHOE 'DO'S

Keep it simple, classic and clean. If in doubt, new, understated trainers and a bit of attitude are fine (though not for classy black-tie dos, obviously). Leave attention-grabbing footwear to the girls.

Finishing Touches
Aftershave

A minefield. It's far worse to have too much aftershave on than none – in fact, none is a pretty good rule unless you have it on good authority, i.e. a woman's, that a particular brand is attractive. Studies show that on the whole, men's cologne actually *decreases* blood flow to the vagina, so be warned. That new bottle of scent from the market ain't gonna make her horny: just the opposite, in fact.

A quick note about fake pheromones: in 2005, fake pheromones hit the US in a big way – for men and women. Pheromones are chemicals produced by the body that are said to transmit messages to others, e.g. 'I'm up for it', 'I fancy you', 'You want me'. Paris Hilton was said to be adding them to her perfume and one manufacturer of the formula was urging us to 'think of it as charisma in a bottle'. Heady stuff, then.

Personal testimonies from users, claimed the manufacturers, were along the lines of girls saying, 'I don't know what it is about you, but ...' and of course these girls were much more attractive than any the men had pulled before.

Buyers were urged not to put too much on – because you could be intimidating to the girl you were trying to attract. You should wear it the first time you met them, went the advice, although there were reports of previously platonic female friends starting to sniff around their male mates in an altogether different way. And it was claimed that people in long-term relationships had experienced an improvement in their sex lives.

But buyer, beware! Pheromones work differently on different people. If, for example, your product contains androstenone, but you are one of those who can't smell it, you may be tempted to spray on more. Don't – to everybody else it smells of pee!

Earring
A very hard look to pull off. Ask yourself what you're trying to achieve here. Is it something grown-up and will women perceive it as such? The toughest boy in school? A wannabe pirate? A rock star? Why do men do it? Is it like facial piercings in general – i.e. for people convinced deep down that their faces are a bit boring? Or have you had too much time on your own with only a pin for company? Serving time in a prison or without friends? You see where this is going and why? A smooth, hole-free ear lobe, that's where.

Jewellery in General
Danger. Can occasionally be carried off, but consult a classy woman first.

Glasses

It's the little touches that do things for a man. The right glasses can do a lot, so don't ever skimp here. When you're buying, get it right. Trail around shops for as long as it takes and ask, ask, ask the advice of women if you're not sure yourself. What better way to detract from the fact that you're just one steaming mountain of hormones waiting to erupt than a pair of glasses that say, 'I'm a bit of a catch but you may have to drag me away from being creative/intellectual if you want this to go any further'? Works every time.

Pulling Your Partner

She's seen you in your ropiest underwear and nursed you when you've been ill. If familiarity hasn't bred contempt, then it certainly hasn't kept the flame of passion burning as brightly as you'd like. Is this retrievable? Assuming the vestiges of attraction are in there somewhere, of course it is. She may have seen you look like shit; that doesn't mean she won't notice when you don't. Here are some grooming issues that may be causing coolness between you:

- Wearing the same underwear and socks day after day.
- Not washing your hair.
- Wearing the same clothes most of the time.
- Never showing an interest in getting new clothes.
- Not changing if you go out together – worse still, if you do when you go out without her ...
- ... yet criticizing her clothes and expecting her to dress up for you.

The solution? Don't drag your feet on keeping clean. To put it bluntly, if you smell she's not going to want to cuddle up close. If your bits reek, she's not going to want them anywhere near her. Instead, be clean. Be at least vaguely interested in your appearance. Suggest an evening out where the two of you dress up to the nines and paint the town red. Wear something different for a change – even her fantasy-man get-up, if you're feeling really daring. If she gets home from work early to find you in your gladiator outfit checking your emails, you may just get a sympathy shag out of it.

Before You Go Out: Checklist

We've covered the basics – you're ready to be let loose. But will you remember all these words of wisdom when the time comes to make your move? Possibly not. So here's a handy checklist that summarizes it all for you.

Have you:

1. Shaved, showered and washed your hair?

2. Cut your fingernails? (They should be clean and short, but not bleeding.)

3. Applied deodorant to stop any sweat patches?

4. Put on clean underwear?

5. Slipped into a stylish shirt?

6. Brushed your teeth? Take some chewing gum with you too, for minty fresh breath at a moment's notice.

7. Done a condom check on your wallet? Remember the old Boy Scout motto: be prepared.

8. Got some cash? Not that I'm suggesting you pay for sex, but she wouldn't object to a drink or two.

9. Stocked up on your business cards? These are for handing out to all those luscious ladies you're going to meet. Fiction or non-fiction, the choice is yours ...

10. Assumed a confident – but not cocky – attitude? You da man. Believe it.

All sorted? Then let's get going. You've got some women to seduce, my friend.

III
Choosing Your Hunting Ground: Part One

Get this: the whole world is your hunting ground. You can meet women anywhere, any time. Every girl you encounter has the potential to be your next bedfellow. A thought like that is damn near intoxicating, isn't it?

Some hunting grounds are a little more obvious than others, though. Bars, clubs, parties, speed-dating nights, dating sites: these are modern meccas for the on-the-prowl lad. So here is the low-down on the most blatant places to hunt your prey, as well as tips on how to maximize your chances in each venue.

On the Dance Floor

So, it's Friday night and you are out on the pull. You've never been so up for it. How to guarantee success?

If you're approaching a group of girls in a club, don't be the slimy old guy in a suit sliding in to dance with us. If there are a bunch of us girls together, we're having a perfectly good time already. We don't need you to complete our evening. However, a sly snog always goes down well as a side order. You've just got to strike a balance between coming across as a toadying twat, and being someone fun to spend time with.

41

BEFORE WE BEGIN, A NOTE ON HUNTING IN PACKS

Wherever you are, in whatever venue, *avoid this like the plague*. Nobody is attracted to it. Ever seen the fear in the eyes of the lone schoolboy at the bus stop when the gang of schoolgirls are all cackling loudly for his benefit? Perhaps you've been that boy. Packs of wolves baying for blood don't get the juices flowing. They're either threatening or worthy of a 'Hmmph, bloody kids' eye roll. Think how many times you've managed to pull on a stag night (snogging a paid lap dancer doesn't count). Funnily enough, girls aren't attracted to a gang of guys all competing with each other to be the lairiest, loudest and drunkest bloke there. We like a bit of personal attention.

By far the safest option is to go out hunting with a wingman. You know the drill. He's there as a physical embodiment of your popularity ('Look, I have a friend and am a socially well-adjusted guy'); to take away the cringe factor of approaching a girl solo ('I'm not making a beeline for you, my buddy and I just thought it would be cool to hang out with you girls for a while'); plus you can share the crop between you. Result.

Dance floor tips:

- Appear confident and smiley.
- Be chatty if you like, but entertain yourself because she can't hear a word you're saying – unless there's a sudden break in the music or a power cut and you're left shouting: 'Nice tits!'

- Bump into girls because the rhythm's gotcha – but don't bump too hard and do say sorry with a big, winning smile.
- If she's so irresistible you seriously can't keep your hands off her, opt for a gentle fingertips-only hold on her hips. Never grind your hard-on into her back and avoid the arse grope. If she firmly removes your hands wherever you touch her, she's not interested. Move on.
- If she smiles, don't take that as your cue to slap down the piece of cardboard you picked up in the supermarket car park on the way and start experimenting with throwing break-dancing shapes. Smile back.
- Keep your moves simple rather than getting too ambitious – don't do the splits unless you can, and even then retain a sense of humour: you're trying to get laid, not land a part in *Fame*.

The Student Bar

Provider of some of the easiest lays of your life. Everyone's giddy with excitement at being away from home for the first time; they're flush with the privacy and liberation of having a room they can use for sex which *isn't* under their parents' roof; they subconsciously know they're young and foolish and can put any mistakes down to experience. The student bar isn't the haunt of savvy twenty-somethings or the cynical thirty-plus: instead, it's full of hot, young, ambitious optimists, always on the lookout for the next sexual high and new experience. Cash in on the moment and all those raging hormones – you'll never have it so good again.

To optimize your chances, get a basic level of hygiene – see 'Hey, Good Lookin''. Don't have smelly feet, one pair of boxer shorts and a hovel for a room. Your chances will already tower over those of 97 per cent of other students.

The Country Pub

This deserves a category all of its own because of the kind of girls you'll find here: country bumpkin lasses. They have an earthy appeal because:

- They're up for it – there's nothing to do in the countryside except have sex and watch animals having sex. So she knows the ropes. She won't be shy.
- You're providing the entertainment. Not only is there nothing to do in the countryside, the available pool of men is very small. By the time she reached her late teens, she'd got through all the men in the area. She's now looking to pastures new. Any old pastures – including you.

Approach them with:
- Car keys – perhaps for a sports car rather than a tractor.
- News of all the exciting things that go on in town and how you're a part of that.
- A vague knowledge of country affairs: tree, bird, etc.

Friends of Friends

Have you been making the most of your female friends?
No, not by being fuck-buddies with them all, shagging
whenever you're both single and need a quick pick-me-up
– I mean by exploiting their contacts and friendships. You
can't do it in too overt a way, obviously. No woman would
pimp her mates in such a heartless fashion. But you'll find
that she's more than willing to set up blind dates with
them, so long as she doesn't seriously want you for herself,
of course. If she likes you, you won't get a look-in with her
mates.

Check out your Rolodex or that little black book. Who
are your female friends and what might their friends be
like? Foxy ladies usually have foxy friends – it's that old
Darwin effect again: the strong seek out the strong and
bond (that doesn't mean lesbo action, by the way). So,
even if you don't fancy getting it on with a particular girl,
she could have mates you'd die to make sweet love to.
Befriending an attractive woman could lead to a whole
new network of potential pulls courtesy of her friendship
group. Be a charming, down-to-earth, all-round nice guy.
Casually mention your career prospects (job, salary, car,
etc.). Make her laugh. She'll have them queuing up for you
without you having to lift a finger.

Don't forget your male mates either. They could have a
whole harem of beautiful bezzie mates that you've not yet

plundered. How to meet these friends of friends? Well, there's the aforementioned blind date – or there's the house party.

How to Give Good House Party

> # Girl Talk
> *'The guy who's having the party is already quite attractive for being the party-giver. He's got power.'*

Where's the most obvious place to meet new women? At a party. Not being invited to enough? Throw your own. Only one rule if you want to ensure quality guests: get it talked about beforehand. Frankly, if you're not top of everyone else's invitation list, you alone might not be the biggest draw in town. You need a gimmick, a rumour to get put around. It doesn't need to be true, but if it's not, make sure the big event is happening long after everyone's too drunk to remember:

- 'Did you know Johnny Depp is his cousin? He and Vanessa Paradis are dropping by around midnight with her band and they're going to play a set.'
- 'The Ritz's head cocktail waiter is his brother-in-law! Apparently he's coming over after work to mix diamond Martinis for a couple of hours.'

Of course, with your own party you can:
- Choose the company, the music and the booze.
- Have an excuse to keep flirting with everyone until the last minute and hedge your bets. It's your job! You're the host!

- Have a monopoly on the bedroom.
- Make her feel singled out by 'quitting this crazy scene' and taking her out on the roof terrace or balcony or wherever to 'see the view'.
- Decide when it's time for everyone to go home so that you can concentrate on the two-person party about to take place under your duvet.
- Have an excuse to get rid of everyone – including her – hastily in the morning. You've got to tidy up and anyway, you add with touching regret, all good things must come to an end.

Case Study: Chris

'I'd just moved into a new place and decided to throw a massive house-warming. I emailed everyone I knew and asked them to bring everyone *they* knew, so it was quite a big bash. My mate's sister turned up with a friend in tow, Lucy. She was hot: dark hair and really seductive brown eyes. I went over and got them all drinks, and we started chatting. Then something kicked off in the other room and I had to go over and sort it out: I ended up chucking these two gatecrashers out of the house. I could tell Lucy liked that – she got really touchy-feely after that. A bit later, she asked if there was anywhere quieter we could go – she said the music was getting a bit loud. *She* led *me* into the bedroom – and we gave it quite a christening ...'

Dinner Parties

The classier version of the house party: just as much booze, but conducted in a more intimate setting.

- Choose the guest list carefully. Throw in a few blokes – but no one who's going to show you up – or the girls will realize your ploy even before dinner is served. Invite good-natured couples with matchmaking aspirations – but not ones who'll row and ruin the romantic air. Request the pleasure of the company of a good clutch of single girls: not only does it give you more choice, it's less obvious who your main target is.
- Keep the food simple. Prepare as much as possible in advance: it gives you more time to chat her up.
- Hold off from letting her know she's being hit on until the second or third course.
- Even if another guy's steaming in – and you're reminding yourself not to invite *him* again – remember you're still top dog if it's your party.
- Serve generous measures of after-dinner liqueurs – and keep them coming.
- Then it's just a matter of distracting her until the last potential lift has gone, then offering her your bed as you'll 'sleep on the sofa'. Course you will ...

WLTM

Sometimes the party scene isn't enough to secure a shag, however. Perhaps you get nervous and can't capitalize on the all-drinking, all-pulling atmosphere. Maybe girls don't get your dance moves. Whatever, there is another, obvious, option that shouldn't be discounted in your quest to get laid.

Personal Ads and Online Lovin'

As every metropolitan media type knows, the stigma of both personal ads and cyberdating has almost completely gone now. Indeed, many attractive but busy people are reliant on them for their sex lives. More and more magazines and newspapers are having to face the fact that people are looking to their classified pages for sex as well as love.

Whether they are online or in print, there is a knack to writing personal ads. They must not be too honest, mused journalist Euan Ferguson in *The Observer*, rejecting: 'Alcoholic Scots dwarf. Financial shambles. Credit blacklisted on, at the last count, seven continents. Hanging on to job by skin of teeth. Tend to let people down. Eat about once a week, and then unhealthily. Would like to meet easily impressed slut.'

But help is at hand. There are rules about this sort of thing. Here are a few tips that should get the ladies interested:

- **Get a good headline**. You may find that the cocky ones meet with success: 'Last of the Good Ones Not Taken – Yet'; 'Great Catch Going to Waste'. Others prefer a more self-deprecating take. Ferguson spotted: 'Monocled, plaid-festooned gadabout, out of place in any relationship or century.' But this strikes me as risky.
- **Describe yourself first** – rather than writing a long list of 'wants'.
- **Apply your own rules to your description**. What would you want to know about someone else?
- **Be specific**. Not just 'enjoys movies and eating out', but 'Tarantino and Thai restaurants'; not just 'likes music', but 'The Strokes and Shakira'.
- **Be honest** – but not ridiculously so, don't talk about

your problem with commitment or your emotional baggage. If it's sex you're after, mention 'fun and frolics'. They'll get the message.

- **Mention your age**. Include this, or at least an age range – 'early thirties', 'mid-forties'. It won't put people off as much as you may think.
- **Be creative**. If not a poem, then an entire advert in song titles, perhaps? And show, don't tell. If you reckon you've got a GSOH, be funny. Women are suckers for classy men, too: is there a literary quote that describes you particularly well?
- Above all, *don't lie* – it's silly. What's the point? You'll get found out straight away.

Case Study: Caroline

Caroline was very excited about meeting a guy she'd seen and got to know on an online dating site. She got her hair done, bought some new clothes and travelled the length of the country to meet him, arranging to stay with friends who didn't live too far away.

And when she met him? He wasn't him. He had put a photograph of someone else up on his web page. Caroline stumbled through the date, with both of them ignoring the elephant in the room. Eventually they parted. Then she stayed with her friends and headed back home, totally deflated.

'What did he look like?' her mates all asked. She managed to summon up a mental picture of him. He wasn't a bad-looking guy, she conceded, but she had no idea whether she would have fancied him or not, because she couldn't get past the deceit.

Speed Dating

Unless you're signing up for some very high-class speed dating, you'll learn pretty quickly that the room is likely to be full of gorgeous girls dressed up to the nines (oh yes!) and men trying less hard. Perhaps you're attracted to the 'speed' part of the dating because it sounds like less effort than a real date. You can perfect a two-minute repertoire pretty easily and then just keep repeating it. For commitment-phobes, it's the ideal event: one evening, twenty different girls.

The difficulty being, of course: one evening, twenty different suitors competing for the very same ladies. And the competition can be fierce. How to stand out? Arm yourself with a few choice questions and recycle. And remember, like you, we just wanna have fun. *Everyone* at these events wants to pull. It's why they're there. It's not like clubbing, where it's pot luck as to who's up for it and who's already taken, and you're just as likely to get shot down as to score. This audience is willing and able. So make the most of it. Turn on the charm. Blow the other suckers out of the water, and make sure it's plain sailing when it comes to reaping the rewards of your two-minute routine.

Some Questions

Stuck for things to say speed dating? Not used to asking a woman about herself? Make yourself memorable. A recent speed-dating experiment showed that one guy and one girl in their sample of twenty managed a 100-per-cent hit rate. How? They were not more than averagely attractive physically, but they asked left-field questions: 'Which pizza topping do you favour?' 'If you were on *Stars in Their Eyes*, who would you be?'

So keep it quirky, energetic and open-ended:

- 'Tell me something no one else knows about you.'
- 'What's your earliest memory?'
- 'Which famous people, living or dead, would you invite to your fantasy dinner party? You're allowed six.'
- 'How would your best friend describe you?'
- 'What was the last thing that made you laugh?'
- 'What was the last thing that made you cry?'
- 'Run me through your life in one minute.'
- 'Run me through your day in one minute.'
- 'Which famous person would you most like to go for a drink with?'
- 'What's the best meal you've ever eaten? Where were you?'
- 'If money were no object, what would you do tomorrow?'

Good luck!

||||
Hunting, Gathering and Getting Laid

Where do most of us spend the vast majority of our waking hours? At work. So it stands to reason that, however tame and limited it may seem as a backdrop to your exploits, the workplace is actually your prime hunting ground. You have to be clever, though, in order to create a thrilling chase among the mundane day-to-day of office life – amid the printer paper and the Post-it notes. Having said that, the real aficionado in this field can, cannily, choose his job on the basis of its pick-up potential.

Top Ten Pulling Professions

10 Lifeguard. Daily opportunities here for saving scantily clad lovelies, clearly.

9 Bouncer. Doors aren't the only thing this job opens ... Think smart suits, *Men-in-Black*-style chic and access-all-areas passes. Whether you're the gateway to a boy band or a hot new club, girls will be desperate to get on your good side.

8 Gardener. All that lovely, posh, desperate-housewife totty. Who knows? If she can afford to pay for a gardener, she might even pay you for sexual favours.

7 Yachtsman. Invite her for adventures on the high seas and comfort her when those same seas get choppy. You take control and steer, she gets to lie in front of you in a bikini all day and get more and more tanned, bringing you the occasional gin and tonic when the sun's over the yardarm.

6 Actor. It is, after all, virtually written into the contract to get it on with your co-star, regardless of the marital status or level of celebrity of either of you. If you doubt your talents will get you to the heady heights of Angelina, why not consider taking up amateur dramatics? (See page 66.) It doesn't come with a million-dollar pay cheque, but the totty can be just as tasty.

5 Tennis coach. Think about it. All that standing behind distracted women in short skirts with your arms around them, showing them how to grip the shaft and serve a blinder. It's a no-brainer.

4 Barman. An obvious one, but think of all those tipsy women. Cocktail-making ability dramatically increases success rate. The barman also benefits from the 'shoulder-to-cry-on' syndrome: when women are drowning their break-up blues with a large bottle of Chardonnay, a man's just got to be in the right place at the right time to show them not all men are bastards. Women, eternal optimists, always think, 'Maybe *this* time ...'

3 Porn star. Not so much a pulling profession, because no pulling is necessary: the job is getting laid. Perhaps one for those who are too lazy for the challenge of the chase. The challenge here is getting and keeping it up on demand.

2 Chief executive. It barely matters of which company: power is the aphrodisiac. Works best if you've a huge office with spectacular views and a big strong desk (perfect for bending her over on to – and yes, she'll be thinking the same), but if you're lacking in these resources somewhat, a couple of mocked-up business cards might do the job just as well.

1 Fireman. Reassuringly, you don't even need to be a particularly good fireman. Or, indeed, a genuine one. Just wear the uniform and grasp that big hose of yours, and women will be flinging themselves at you before you can say, 'Fire, police or ambulance?'

How to Get From Your Desk to Down and Dirty

Those who work from home are at a distinct disadvantage for this ploy: you never meet anyone by the water cooler or the overheating photocopier. However, spend just a couple of days, or even hours, of your working week away from your desk, and that hunting ground widens once more. How about taking your laptop on a scouting expedition? Try a relaxed coffee bar or the library, and check out the chicks as you're checking your emails.

For the rest of us, everybody knows that offices are hotbeds of sexual tension: all those bored people in one place letting their minds wander as they look upon others for whom they don't have to make meals or wash underwear. Offices are places for keeping your mind off the job you're paid to do and on *the* job – usually with several co-workers simultaneously. And don't even get me started on the catalyst effect of a residential conference ...

So, everyone's exchanging sly, seductive looks from behind their computer screens. You need to stand out from the crowd and get yourself noticed – for the right reasons. In the workplace, where we all present a vaguely professional veneer, women won't just be swayed by your clothes or the manner in which you close a deal: they'll be looking beyond all that to try to suss out who you really are. Be ready for them.

What Your Desk Says About You

Little furry animals? Photographs of women you've been with or would like to go with? No, no, no. Bits of sandwich and empty coffee cups everywhere? Would we sleep with this man? Are you out of your mind? Would it even be hygienic to do so?

On the other hand, very neatly stacked piles of paper placed in carefully labelled 'In' and 'Out' boxes? Will his piece of work be going in and out anywhere near a ladies' region? Of course not. The man's clearly a serial killer.

For once, I think mediocrity is the watchword here. A couple of piles of ongoing work, a big important-looking package with your name on it, and possibly signs of a life being led outside the office – a tennis ball or a copy of *Time Out* that is, not an alligator or a quad bike parked up next to your desk.

Nailing Your Boss

All of the above applies – unless you want to nail your boss. That's a whole different ball game. You're seeking to impress, but not to ingratiate. To stand out, but not to get above your station.

Male bosses have been shagging their secretaries as a matter of course/out of politeness for decades – but this isn't the case for the ladies. You can't fall back on years of tradition, so how do you pull her?

The answer: work hard. It's different with a female boss. It's not enough for you to look good and look adoringly into her eyes, or wear a lot of make-up and a short skirt and sit on her knee. Apply yourself. Get the work done on time or early, but present it to her after hours. Volunteer for projects that will necessitate working late into the night together. Once the assignment's finished, gently suggest a celebratory drink. As you get to the end of the bottle of champagne, mention the importance of champagne in life. Her partner/ex may have been too mean to buy champagne. This gives you the seductive upper hand. Be gentlemanly with a touch of class. Remember she's intelligent, or she wouldn't have got to where she is. Flatter her mind. Compliment her achievements. Emphasize how much you respect her. Next stop – your place, and your turn to show her who's boss.

Case Study: Jim

'I was going through a bit of a drought when Maria started work at the company. I noticed her straight away – good body, redhead, infectious laugh. I made my move immediately – but subtly. Didn't want to get shot down in front of everyone. I'd send her the odd email, just to check she was "settling in okay", and she really responded to it. We'd have a bit of banter flying back and forth all day, then when I saw her in the canteen or wherever she'd flash me a smile and we'd have a chat. One night, we were the last ones left in the pub. With all the flirting that had been going on, what happened next seemed inevitable. I got some more drinks in, we moved closer and closer together as the night wore on and we ended up snogging. A few more nights like that and then we closed the deal. It was great the next day in the office. We knew exactly what we'd been getting up to the night before, but all our colleagues were in the dark. It was such a huge turn-on – we were all over each other again come 5.30.'

How to Get the Girl From Accounts Without Getting Your Marching Orders

As Bertrand Russell put it: 'No one gossips about someone's secret virtues.' Nothing gets round an office faster than a reputation – not emails, not internal mail, not even word of someone getting fired or being pregnant. So discretion has to be the order of the day.

Getting laid in the workplace is not the domain of the bragger. The bragger will soon be without not only women to have sex with, but also a pay cheque at the end of the month.

Nor will the complete laggard get laid in the workplace. There's nothing sexy about someone who's work-shy. Can't be arsed to make a deadline? You're hardly going to be giving your all to finding my G spot, are you?

Almost as important is to be the dude who stays out of office politics. No one likes a schemer. Least of all the schemers themselves.

How to Put the 'X' Back into Office Xmas Parties

Drunken superiors; manky little bits of proffered mistletoe; eighties hits on a small, inferior stereo in the corner; saucy secret-Santa gifts; cheap warm Chardonnay; shivering on the steps outside with a badly rolled joint. Ah, the joys of office parties ...

These dubious social gatherings are thought of as the very last word in banality and misery – but this can be capitalized on. If she's miserable, your efforts are only going to cheer her up! The trick is to get her away from the Pringles and move the nibbling into the meeting room. Cliché or no, it is a turn-on to do it in the workplace. If your pretext for stealing her away from the 'action' is that you want to 'show her something' (unimaginative, but might just do the job if the party's dismal), ensure that it's not a report you've just finished, a pornographic email or a photocopy of an arse – yours or anyone else's.

Xmas party etiquette:

- Make your move when you won't be missed. It's no good peaking early and whisking her away before the sit-down meal with the table plan. Everyone will still be sober enough at that stage to put two and two together when you don't turn up for the prawn cocktail starters and the turkey dinner.

- Let her know you're interested. I'm not talking a fly-past by the Red Arrows or an ad in *The Times*, but some subtly placed significant looks and smiles will plant the seeds of seduction better than any gardener could. Compliment her, laugh at her jokes. Most importantly: always make sure her glass has something in it, and chivalrously offer to fetch her another warm white wine if she's running low. If she's aware of your affection, her drink-fuddled brain will automatically turn to you when the last dance of the night comes round and she needs a partner.

- Perhaps surprisingly, dirty dancing is normally allowed at office parties – even actively encouraged by managers, who seem to enjoy seeing their staff so patently bonding. So grind away, but watch the exploring hands: rubbing your bits together rhythmically is permissible, grabbing her tits is usually frowned upon.

- Secrecy is key. It's not going to look good for either of you at your next appraisal if your boss saw you making out under the mistletoe. Don't feed the gossip if you can help it. Suspicion is one thing; cold hard evidence (usually taken by some enterprising nerd on the company's digital camera, and emailed round on the Monday morning) is ten times worse. So be the last two at the party; or head off together to a 'better' venue; or subtly sneak off to the loos for a quickie, one later than the other and returning the same way ... but keep the canoodling out of sight.

A Sober Word of Warning

Office fantasies – indulged in 9–5.30 on a regular basis – are wonderful, because they don't ask anything of us. Before actually embarking on getting laid in the office, ensure that you really want your thoughts to become a reality of some kind – and that all the signs are there for you to make your move. That hot girl in marketing may be driving you to distraction; she may also drive you out of a job with a sexual harassment case if you don't watch your back. And what if it works out? Six months down the line, are you going to be happy seeing her day in, day out and every night as well – without even the possibility of some light-hearted office flirtation with another colleague to break the monotony? What happens if you have a one-night stand ... and go in the next day to find everyone snickering behind their computers? What if she dumps you? What if you dump her? It's all so complicated ...

Having said that, there are fewer things more delicious than a secret love affair conducted via saucy emails and quickies in the stationery cupboard, all orchestrated under the noses of other colleagues who seem blissfully unaware of the bubbling, boiling sexual tension that's being cooked up in between team meetings. Go for it.

꒐꒐꒐꒐

Choosing Your Hunting Ground: Part Two

Okay, so we've covered the basics. But bars and speed dates and meeting people at work are, in all honesty, the choices of lazy amateurs. For surprising sex, for unconventional coupling, you've got to think outside the box. Don't restrict yourself to pubs and clubs – with such a limited hunting ground, no wonder you're not getting laid. If you haven't found a date by being out on the pull overtly, widen your horizons. Open your eyes to the world around you. Nobody said your enticement territory had to be specifically engineered towards snaring your prey; use your everyday life to change your luck. Join a gym, or an evening class, or some other innocuous activity. Find fruit from doing the things you actually like doing – going to gigs, whatever. Libraries are full of sexual tension; kickboxing classes are sweaty, physical, fun; galleries and book signings are stimulating.

The key point is: your prey will be unsuspecting and you will be king of the jungle. Think like James Bond. Go undercover. No longer are you the eligible young bachelor openly stalking your sweetheart on the dance floor. You've got to be more subtle than that – I promise, she'll be swept off her feet.

This chapter contains dozens of alternative suggestions for meeting women – so get stuck in and get out there. Let's dive head first into this mind-blowing menagerie ...

The Gym

Let's get this straight: the gym is not a place to get fit, it's a place to get fit women. I bet you love all that skintight Lycra gear. Doesn't her body look great all glistening with sweat like that? Are you the one to give her a *real* workout? But wait: an important tip for pulling in the gym is *not* to perve at the scantily clad senoritas. Of course we know you're checking us out as we work ourselves into a sweat, panting heavily in the process, our breasts rising and falling as our pulses race ... but we're not particularly comfortable with the idea of you getting off on it, okay? Interaction is the key. Talk to us. Put us at our ease. Make like you're making conversation rather than just making a move.

How about joining a mixed martial-arts class? As one of the few guys in it (probably), you'll no doubt be called upon for class demonstrations. The prospect of fifteen women confidently straddling you one after the other sounds like a good deal to me. Just think of all the physical contact. You're most of the way there already ...

Suggested lines:
- 'I'd like you to sweep me off my feet.'
- 'Perhaps we could partner up for this exercise?'
- 'I think we should try that one more time.'

The Ultimate Foreplay Sport

Speaking of fitness, how about taking up horse riding? Let's see ... It's full of fit, posh women wearing clothes that show off their curves. There's daily contact with the language of lust – 'riding', 'straddling', 'champing at the bit', 'getting your leg over', 'flat out', 'tally ho' – and plenty of opportunity for extended periods of outdoor intimacy where you can dazzle her with your skills, sensitivity and wit. Sounds like a plan.

On the plus side for the female race, you'll be fitter and emerge from your new hobby with a great arse.

Gigs and Festivals

'If music be the food of love, play on ...' Gigs and festivals: home to the rock chick and the New Age hippie.

Rock chicks have a kind of grungy appeal because:
- They're loyal, but don't expect anything in return (all those nights spent in training backstage as band member X decided which groupie to have that night).
- They will put up with all kinds of bad behaviour with a cute, tolerant smile.
- They're filthy and eager to please in bed.

Approach them with:
- A ready knowledge of who's hot and who's not on the rock scene and why. A quick scan through any edgy rock mag should be enough to achieve this.
- The ability to play three chords on a guitar.

New Age hippies, on the other hand, have a flaky appeal. You'll also find this chick on wacky evening courses: 'Beginners' Reiki', a 'Crystal Healing Workshop', 'Uses for Runes' and so on. If you're really resourceful, you'll select a course that enables you to target only desperate, available New Agers: 'Love Spells and How to Apply Them';

'Auras and Moving On'; 'Awakening Your Magick Love Goddess', etc. Hippies are good girls to try it on with because:

- They're gullible. Tell them that the rude thing you want to do to them on the first night is known to unlock their chakras and release potent spiritual energy (or whatever) and they'll be putty in your hands.
- They're up for it – some witch (or canny wizard) told them years ago that being free with their sexuality was the key to enlightenment and tapping into the universal power, and they've been as free as possible with it ever since.

Approach them with:
- Three balls in the air.
- A few vaguely plausible ways of interpreting their dreams.
- A cocktail-party knowledge of palm reading.
- A spliff.

Amateur Dramatics

This might be worth a shot. After all, you'll be the only straight man in the cast, and the women are likely to be frustrated actresses who don't get to express all that creativity and inner passion any other way. That's where you come in, helping them to channel their excess energy. You have to play the long game with this one – the cast party after the show is the pinnacle to this pulling ploy. Learn lines together in the pub; calm her first-night nerves in the wings; help her work off that post-performance high in an intimate dressing room, surrounded by lilies and with the sound of applause still ringing in her ears.

Best of all, land the role of the leading man. Everyone knows the sexual tension brewing between the main actors eventually reaches boiling point. And just think of the kissing practice, the topless sex scenes: all achieved without you having to think up your own chat-up lines (some playwright's already done the job for you). And that's not all – come opening night, everyone in the audience will fancy you too.

Suggested lines:
- 'But soft, what light through yonder window breaks? It is the east and Juliet is the sun.'
- 'Can I help you with your greasepaint?'

Spanish Salsa

The problem with salsa and Spanish lessons – unless you actually want to learn to salsa or speak Spanish – is that women are starting to think of these as clichés, such that by going you are effectively saying, 'I want to get laid, but I've run out of ideas of my own about how to do it.'

This from Marie, who's tried: 'You might as well say, "Fancy a shag? I'm available." In our local town there are salsa dancing classes and a bunch of us girls from work went. Never again. It was packed to the rafters with old men wanting sex. Literally, desperate over-fifties.'

The trick, then, is to seem really into your salsa.

Suggested lines:
- 'Can I help you with your Floor Sweep Whip?'
- 'I'm going to make you a copy of this CD by little-known Argentinian musician José Cuervera ... I think it matches the way you move.'

Card Sharks

Why not learn how to play poker? Find a complicit bar and a couple of friends who are keen to join you – at least one of whom is female – and the rest will follow. Everyone fancies themselves a card shark these days. And once you've mastered the game, you're in a position to teach willing females, offering intimate lessons where you show them the ropes.

In taking up cards, you may even earn some money. You could become a high-stakes player, travelling to Las Vegas to win millions of dollars. Just think how many fit women hang around those sorts of tournaments. You'll also find that those millions of dollars (even the potential of them) drastically increase your eligibility, too. I can't think why that would be.

Suggested lines:
- 'To start with, why don't you watch me get into it with my hand, and then you can take over from me?'
- 'I'm on my way to Vegas, baby, yeah! Fancy tagging along for the ride of your life?'

The Library

Home to the bookworm: the tastiest morsel that ever quoted Tennyson. Female bookworms are hot because:
- They get overlooked by others – so you don't have to fight through hordes of other guys to get to her.
- The Reveal. There may be that 'Why, you're beautiful!' moment when you take down her hair and remove her glasses.
- They're up for it. All that reading about it, but not doing it, has got to have an effect on a girl's libido. It's always the quiet ones, isn't it?

Approach them with:

- A few choice quotations.
- An air of worldly wisdom that speaks to them of knowing all about the real world, the world outside of books.
- But still an apparent appreciation of their need for intellectual stimulation (whatever).

Case Study: Emma

'I was in the library last week and saw a classic example of a man going wrong by being too obvious. There was a guy almost opposite me who was clearly hitting on an attractive blonde in a stripy scarf, but she upped and left. Why? Because he sat next to her. If you're picking up girls in this way, you've got to approach them obliquely – literally. Sit obliquely opposite. Don't make it obvious. Think about it for a second: who – apart from a creepy stalker – would sit right next to someone they fancied in a library?'

A New Leaf

Not necessarily staged in a library, but a method of similar literary ilk: the book group (especially fruitful if you can be bothered to get to the end of a novel or two). You won't automatically be pulling middle-aged, bookish ladies, you know. There are groovy, sexy book groups these days that are full of young women, especially in metropolitan areas. You might need to develop your networking skills, however, in order to hear about them in the first place and then be invited to join in (it's a bit like the Masons or a threesome that way).

Suggested lines:
- 'I'm worried about the inner emotional life of the main protagonist in this novel. He seems so unthinking and one-dimensional!'
- 'I think the book would have been much more successful if one of its main female characters had been written as a real, complex human being. The author hasn't been fair to his women at all.'

Beauty and Brains

If it's a cultivated lay you're after, you might try those singles evenings in art galleries. How about a wine-tasting weekend if you want to increase your style factor and meet drunk women along the way? Or join the Friends of the nearest city library and go to their evening talks.

Suggested lines:
- 'Unless I'm very much mistaken, that's Minoan script on that tablet. It famously inspired Ventris to decipher Linear B.'
- 'What do you think of this wine? Can you taste pencil lead? Not sure that I can ...'

If even these suggestions leave you lonely (or if you've exhausted all the bounty on offer – down, boy), it's time to think again. You'll need superb casing-the-joint skills, for you must now be prepared to look for lovers in the most unusual places. Your antennae must be red-hot, quivering with questing passion and ready to plunge into the deepest, darkest corners in search of eligible elixir. Think you can handle it? Then read on ...

Supermarket Sleaze

As anybody who's been into a supermarket when it's dark outside knows, supermarkets in cities can ooze sexual tension. Especially since late-night and all-night opening were introduced, these superstores have become hunting grounds ripe with opportunity. They say that if you see a man on his own in a supermarket, he's single – although if he has a packed trolley and looks tired, presumably he's doing the family shop – so women are already making this assumption about you.

The important thing, obviously, is to carry the right stuff in your basket. So no bulk-buying of cheap lager and potato chips. There are several balances to be struck here: the shopping must not look too sad and lonely and scream 'meal for one'; but if it looks like you're cooking for a lady, you must somehow convey that you haven't committed to her yet. Smile confidingly at the cute shopper beside you in a 'we-gourmets-are-our-own-worst-enemies-aren't-we?' way, as you pick out your artichoke.

Basket candy might include parmesan, parma ham, extra virgin olive oil, sun-dried tomatoes, scallops. Opening gambits might include offering to reach a shelf she can't – but try not to show off about this – and letting her into the queue in front of you because you have more stuff than her.

Other methods:
- The you-have-it-no-you sacrifice: you both reach for the last packet of something or other (it doesn't matter what, as long as it's not piles cream), then you manfully, chivalrously and graciously let her have it. If you can engineer subtle yet actual physical contact in the process (hand brushing hand, rather than your hand brushing her arse, by the way), so much the better.

- The 'accidental' trolley collision (but don't push too hard – you're in a supermarket, not on a rally course).
- The can-you-read-this-label-my-eyes-aren't-great request (said humbly, rather than as though you're an eighty-year-old with cataracts – unless, of course, you are an eighty-year-old with cataracts, in which case I'm not sure even this book is going to help you ...)

Number closing – getting her phone number – is always the difficulty in situations like these, to the extent that many people think pulling in a supermarket is a bit of an urban myth. If you can't make a supermarket sweetheart of her in the time available with a well-placed line, simply hand her your card with a smile that doesn't look like it's just been purchased from the cheese counter.

NB: Just as with pulling barmaids and waitresses, you'll have to pull out something extra special if you want to score with the checkout girl. She's heard it all before and couldn't care less what's in your basket.

Puppy Love

As any dog owner knows, possessing a dog transforms your relationship with the opposite sex and increases your chances of getting laid in three different ways:

1. Via the dog-owning community
2. Via dog-loving passers-by and bystanders
3. Via the children of single parents

How it works is this: you and your dog go out for a walk. (By the way, I'm not suggesting you actually buy a dog – they're for life, not just for pulling girls, you know: you can always borrow one or volunteer for the local dogs' home instead.) The important thing is to be seen out and about with it. It immediately sends out a great message: 'I am a caring, emotionally well-adjusted young man who accepts responsibility. I am at ease with physical contact and give love willingly and readily.' It might all be bollocks: it doesn't matter. It'll get you laid. Another plus point: dog owners are rumoured to be fantastic lovers.

There are some delicate balances to strike. What kind of dog should you be seen with? A pit bull detracts from the whole 'gentle-guy-without-a-violent-bone-in-my-body' veneer. A chihuahua doesn't necessarily say 'gay', but it doesn't do a lot for your masculinity. In general, you want a normal-sized, friendly dog. An ugly one might elicit some sympathy: turn that to your advantage. (NB: You can apply these categories to your human friends, too: it might influence your decision as to whom you'll make your wingman.)

One more thing – watch how your dog behaves with you. It may affect your chances. If he's cowed into submission and looks like he's been beaten, girls will avoid you like the plague, thinking you're a thug. On the other hand, a pet with military discipline makes you look like a control freak who will make love by numbers and not think of it as the creative act it should be; a dog running riot will annoy her and make her think you've got no backbone. Opt for a happy dog who can do some of the essential legwork for you – just try not to get too jealous when she spends more time stroking him than she does you. Your time will come.

This ploy works just as well with babies, too. If you can borrow one – best of all in one of those papoose slings – while you walk around the local park, you'll find that a kid is a natural babe magnet (as long as the child is well-behaved – see above). Be sure to stress you're helping out a friend with the babysitting – not only does it big up your caring, considerate side, but only women with the very darkest of morals will still go for you if they think you're part of a happy family. (NB: Reinventing yourself as a widower for the sympathy vote is a highly risky strategy.)

The False Premise Method

Girl Talk

'Billy and I met when he came round to "look at a room" I was renting. He didn't need a room at all. He was already living somewhere. Then we went for a drink afterwards ... When I was next single, I met Sean when I told him I "needed driving lessons". The fact that I already had my licence must have slipped my mind.'

You see – we do it too. So, engineer meetings with girls through the flimsiest of routes. Why shouldn't you? There are 3 billion women on the planet – you're not going to get the chance to meet them all unless you get off your arse and get to it.

Tips:
- Don't give yourself away too early – continue the role play until you can make your excuses and leave (the landlady who sounded so sexy on the phone might turn out to be a bit different in the flesh, after all), or until you can reveal your true intentions towards her.
- Arrange to meet her in a safe place. It's not just guys that can be psychos, you know.

- Be aware she might not ever want to know the truth. After all, you're starting this relationship (be it a one-night stand or more long-term) on false premises. The whole thing's riddled with deceit. Some girls don't go for that sort of thing, funnily enough.

Case Study: Neil

'I'd had enough of being single. Not just single – celibate. So come New Year, my mate Neil and I decided to do something about it. We placed an ad for language tutors in the local rag. Neil was going for French; I wanted to "learn" Italian. Eventually, we both hooked up with these sexy foreigners for some "one-on-one tutorials". Neil was well prepared, and set by a whole afternoon and evening for his first session. But he was bitterly disappointed: she actually tried to teach him French! Sofia and I, however, got on really well. I wasn't *too* keen, not like Neil: we started off just having the odd lunch together, or we'd meet up for a walk by the river. It turned out that she wanted to improve her English, so I ended up teaching her – in more ways than one, you could say.'

Fun and Frolics at Formal Ceremonies
Weddings

Weddings are like a little holiday from reality, with everybody getting on and wanting the best for the happy couple, which makes them good places to pick up girls. All the rules go out the window at a wedding – which is ironic when you think about it, because they're all about formally imposing restrictions on the bride and groom.

Speaking of whom, let's not forget what the big day's all about. Commitment. Love. Romance. All the female guests will be on heat – they love that stuff! In addition, they'll have spent hours (not to mention hundreds of pounds) on how they look that day, and will be searching high and low for someone to appreciate it.

Case Study: Cally

'I blame the red dress – and the fact that I was on the rebound, having been dumped by someone I was head over heels in love with. At the wedding meal, a guy was sitting on one side of me and his wife was on the other side. He was a bit of a cocky shit at the dinner table and she was a bit snotty and offhand.

'Later on, everyone was dancing. I was drunk and the guy's wife had gone to bed – perhaps they'd had a row, I don't know. The next thing I knew, we were sitting at the bar and he was coming on to me. He was being seductive in the right way – although he did say, "I want to kiss your face off" which is pretty disgusting, come to think of it; "I want to kiss you" would have been fine – and we arranged to meet in the woods outside.

'I jumped out of the window and we copped off in a copse. He pounced on me. It was awful sex and I could feel branches sticking in my back. What can I say? I was emotionally deranged at the time.'

Weddings remind single girls that they're single. By the end of the reception, they'll be drunk, depressed and desperate. Make the most of it. Then there are the women whose partners won't ask them to marry them. They'll be skulking around looking for bouquets to catch. It might be worth making a beeline for one of them: invariably, they'll have had a row with their boyfriend and will be keen to emphasize to him what a bloody good catch they are – this is where you step in, admiring the bloody good catch and seducing her to within an inch of her life. At any rate, all women will be feeling a little emotional, be that emotion happiness, sadness or just plain jealousy. An emotional woman = a reckless woman = happy hunting!

Funerals

You don't necessarily have to be heartless to get it on at a funeral. Again, they're emotional occasions, and girls are crying out to be comforted – sometimes literally. Perhaps funerals provoke some primal urge in us to connect with life, to reassure ourselves that we're still alive; perhaps we turn to each other for solace in sex. Or maybe we're just so oversexed that we are prepared to leap clean over the boundaries of human decency in order to get laid. Whatever, the facts are that you can have some of your hottest sex after funerals. As the film *Wedding Crashers* (2005) has it: 'Grief is nature's aphrodisiac.' Check out those obituaries now.

All too much to take in? Here's my list of:

Top Ten Pulling Places

10 On a long train journey. Unless she wants to get off at a random station in the middle of nowhere, she has nowhere to run but the loos. You helped her put her suitcase up on the rack, so she may as well stick around – if only so that you'll get it down again for her once she's reached her destination.

9 The zoo. Picture the scene: the occasional pair of wild animals rutting; sex in the air; both of you recapturing the breathless, heady excitement of childhood ...

8 Riding stables. The sweaty flanks, the girls in tight trousers – need I say more?

7 On holiday. It doesn't matter where in the world you are, find a fellow holidaymaker and nine times out of ten she'll be receptive to your chat-up line. Ah, the sun, the sangria, the sex on the beach ...

6 Library. In the silence, absorb the sexual tension of all those other readers. Don't worry about a chat-up line beyond 'What's that you're reading?' Knowing a little bit about literature might help to prolong the conversation (unless she's in there for exactly the same reason as you).

5 Massage course. Visions of a thousand nights spent mutually massaging each other in sensual ways are forming in her mind. In fact, you'll probably only have to do it once. For bonus points, swot up on your aromatherapy know-how (see page 117).

4 Hospital. Full of lovely nurses, of course. It's Saturday night, nothing much else is going on for you (the medical staff, on the other hand, will be very busy); you might want to get into a fight or consider a little self-harm to get through the front door. Remember it was the other guy's fault (no one likes a thug); or perhaps you were valiantly protecting a lady's honour (everyone loves a hero). Try not to wince too much at the TCP (wimpish behaviour does not say 'wild in bed').

3 Laundrette. She's already fantasizing about Nick Kamen and that old Levis ad and how much she could do with him during a long spin-cycle – possibly on top of one of the machines ... The windows are steamed up, the air is thick with heat, both of you have got your smalls on display and aren't at all coy about it – get in there, man!

2 Posh chocolate shop. If she sees you agonizing over exactly which Belgian chocolates to choose, she'll think your sexual appetite will be similarly discerning and unhurried (and that you'll buy her chocolates).

1 Themed 'school discos'. She'll already be faint from the nostalgia of it all, remembering snogging Gary Shanklin at the dance in the gym ten or twenty years ago – and she'll be wearing a tiny little school uniform. And I haven't even mentioned the rebellious teenage spirit that'll claim her, telling her to follow her urges recklessly and selfishly and without a thought for the consequences ...

IIII I
Moving in for the Kill

So, you've spotted your gazelle from over the Serengeti that is the nightclub or the library. The adrenaline's started pumping. You're assuming a low, predatory stance, ready to pounce like a panther ... a panther with sweaty palms and his heart in his mouth. A panther who suddenly feels like he's never been on a hunting expedition in his life before. Then you realize you probably look a bit short assuming a low stance, not to mention silly, so you pull yourself together and upright with a small cough. You're as ready as you'll ever be to leap. What's next?

The trick with feeling able to make your move is to get away from the idea that there are those who 'have it' and those who don't. There are only those who have learned to hide their nerves and those who haven't.

She's Interested if ...

The concept of studying body language might appear to take some of the fun and spontaneity out of an encounter. It may even make you – or her if you're staring – feel self-conscious and awkward. On the other hand, as long as you don't tie yourself in knots over it, beginning to notice non-verbal communication where you didn't before can be a fascinating exercise. Not only that: whereas before you might have missed out on chances with girls just because you hadn't learned the language, now you'll be fully fluent at making the most of your animal magnetism.

So, once you've identified a potential pull, casually check out her body language from afar. If she does more than one of the following then the chances are you're in:

- **The four-second checkout.** All but the shyest of us do this, so we are already on the way to being masters of this art. If she's looking steadily at you for longer than she needs to, then she's interested. Don't convince yourself she's not; but for crying out loud don't assume too much either. This is a statement of interest only, not of intent. Don't run over and jump her.

- **The return checkout.** She's looking at you very deliberately again with shiny, up-for-it eyes. One of you is going to have to act sooner or later or the opportunity will be missed. Time to decide whether she's a psycho or a potential partner. How will you play it? Cool and risk the moment passing? Keen and risk having nothing to say? Give it a little while, all the time expressing your interest with glances back in her direction.

- **Touching herself.** No, not like that, you schoolboy. She'll involuntarily touch parts of her body, including her hair and her face, if she fancies you. She might massage her shoulder or even start to remove articles of clothing, the hussy – her jacket, perhaps, or her jumper. It's because, at a primal level, you make her want to be touched. This is a purely animal instinct, though, and not an invitation to dive in. Not yet, for Chrissakes! Not yet ...

- **Blinking when she looks at you.** She's saying, 'It's no coincidence I'm looking in your direction.'

- **The eyebrow lift.** When we see someone we're interested in, our eyebrows shoot up a little. Presumably this is why women shape their eyebrows in that arched way – it's a seduction technique of sorts, just as colouring in our lips or highlighting our eyes are.

Meanwhile, you might find that you're doing the following, subconsciously stating your interest in her:

- **Preening.** If you're smoothing down your clothes, you're showing her that you fancy her by drawing attention to what a catch you are.

- **Pointing towards your crotch with the fingers of both hands** – perhaps with your hands on your hips or thumbs in your pockets. Check out the number of men doing this next time you're in a bar (it's all right, they won't think you're gay). It's remarkable. Clearly, what you're doing here is pointing out the goods on offer to her.

Top Ten Signs You Want Her

10 You're reaching inside your pocket to get your wallet out and buy her a drink.

9 You're salivating.

8 You're getting irritated by your drunken friend's behaviour and comments.

7 You're becoming more aware of other men around you and wondering if you could take them in a fight if they came on to her.

6 You're wondering how much you'd have to pay your flatmate to stay away tonight. Is she worth the price of a hotel room?

5 You're racking your brains trying to remember if you've left any passion-killing artefacts lying about your flat.

4 You're weighing up whether she's worth cancelling tomorrow morning's football training/meeting for – course she is.

3 You're imagining her with fewer and fewer clothes on.

2 In fact, you're starting to imagine fucking her ...

1 You've got a massive hard-on.

NB: A note on girls and their relationships. Look out for previous signs of hurt when you meet a girl. You may be about to open old wounds. Keep away! If you're after a temporary fling – or a permanent thing, come to that – this may be more hassle than it's worth. Telltale signs may be her headlong rush for intimacy or her reluctance to go anywhere near it. This tip may save you from a stalker, suicidal lover or just a hell of a lot of stress. You have been warned.

IS SHE WITH THAT OTHER GUY?

An important consideration. How many times have you crashed and burned because the lady you're after is already attached? Now, if she's on a girls' night out while her boyfriend's tucked up at home in bed, you can be forgiven for making the mistake. But if her fella's in attendance, making a move is not only embarrassing – it can be dangerous. Here's a how-to guide to save you from blushes and black eyes.

You're in a bar and the object of your attention is with another group of people. It's all very confusing. She seems to be hanging around with one other guy in particular. He might be gay for all you know, but you don't want to get into a fight over her. Are they lovers or just friends?

Is she:
- **Always making eye contact with him when she returns to the group?** Or do they otherwise reassure each other, with a touch or a word? If so, you'd better look elsewhere, mate.
- **Holding his hand for extended periods of time?** Likely to be lovers, I'm afraid. Not necessarily particularly secure lovers, those who stick together like glue, but she's probably spoken for nevertheless.
- **Inclining her head towards his?** Bad luck, they're in love.

- **Winding bits of her body round bits of his?** Forget it: she wants him bad.
- **Sitting on his lap?** You might be okay. They're not necessarily lovers. Girls sit on their mates' laps all the time. Does it look territorial or just like she needed a place to sit?

A Woman's Wish List

If a woman's going to sleep with you, she's got to think you're pretty special. So when moving in for the kill it'll help you to know the kind of thing we look out for in a man. Now, everybody's different, but you can't go wrong with a confident, relaxed attitude. A sense of humour is a definite plus. Women, as well as men, base a lot of their perceptions on first impressions. What else have we got to go on, especially if we're meeting a stranger for the first time? So the entrance you make into her ... life should be given just as much consideration as your chat-up line. Be confident in the right way. A wide, genuine smile from the moment you step in the door slays prey and competition alike; fighting and shouting just slay your chances of getting laid. We women – even the most liberal and enlightened of us – are also suckers for a bit of gentlemanly class. So remember these tips to enhance the impression you give.

General gentlemanly behaviour:
- Holding doors open all over the place – sometimes to the extent that you're in the way.
- Offering your seat to a lady.
- Offering to carry whatever the lady is carrying.
- Walking next to the traffic.

- If you're driving – opening the door for her before she gets in and when you arrive at your destination.
- Standing up when a lady leaves the room, and when a lady joins, or leaves, a table. Do it, but subtly, like it's a reflex action. Trust me, she'll be blown away.

Before You Chat Her Up: Checklist

Okay, so she's glanced your way about a hundred times. You've checked behind you and there can be no one else she's looking at. You're about to go over and introduce yourself. But before you do, run your eye down this checklist – it'll help you on your mission, I promise.

1. Is she single? If you skipped the section on page 85, you may be about to get shot down. Make sure she's up for it before you go over.
2. Information/service history. Have you or one of your mates tried to pull her before? Can you incorporate the fact that she works in the record shop in town into your chat-up routine?
3. Chat-up line. Do you know what you're going to say when you get over there, or are you going to play this one by ear, coming up with something off the cuff? Will you say something original, or will one of the oldies-but-goodies be enough to get her where you want her?
4. Breath – does it smell okay? Now might be the time to chew some gum if you're not too sure.
5. Eyeline. Remember to keep it on hers rather than at breast level or over her shoulder at the next available female.

6. Assume a Positive Mental Attitude – you can do this! She's yours for the taking ... but don't go overboard. We like confident, we don't like cocky.

Space Invaders

When a guy chats up a girl, his mission is to get as close to her as possible. He ultimately wants to get so close that 'two become one'. But a girl isn't necessarily clued into this agenda – especially when you first move in for the kill. You have to take things slowly. Get her to trust you. We're back in a body language zone again – but this time you're the one in control. When you first meet a woman, she'll be very protective of her personal space. How to get into hers without making her feel threatened? If you're too 'in her face', you'll be out on your ear. Remember these loose rules instead, and she'll be happily whispering sweet nothings to you before you know it.

The Rules of Informal Space

1 Public (a.k.a. eyeing her up from across the room): 12 feet
2 Social consultative (a.k.a. getting to know her): 4 feet–12 feet
3 Casual-personal (a.k.a. almost close enough to touch): 1.5 feet–4 feet
4 Intimate (a.k.a. Eskimo kisses; you're about to snog her face off): 0–18 inches

Clearly your mission – should you choose to accept it – is to move from 1 to 4 as seamlessly as possible. This is a minefield, but as a general rule, men attempting to seduce women should do so from a range of between 2 and 8 feet, depending on the reception they receive. In other words, guys, don't get too close until she decides that that's her comfort zone.

Body Language – Making It Work for You

All the experts claim that what we say is not the most important thing when it comes to making an impression. Normally, 35 per cent of communication is verbal and 65 per cent non-verbal. In a persuasive situation the value of the words we speak is about 15 per cent of the message (and even less in a noisy bar where the words are lost anyway); speed, tone, pitch, volume and emphasis are about 35 per cent; body movement and eye contact about 50 per cent. What does this mean for your pulling chances? Well, next time you're abroad, remember that you've got just as much chance with the Spanish senoritas as you have with the English chicks. Body language is the international language of love, so don't let your lack of language skills put you off pursuing a promising encounter. All you have to do is get the body language right – here's how.

Some of the most basic body language to watch out for and apply is quite obvious. Do these things to maximize your chances:

- Slow down your movements – no one wants to take a fidget to bed.
- Maintain eye contact – no wandering eyes to see if there's anything better on offer on the other side of the room.
- Smile – to give off a self-assured vibe.

If these few rules put you in a spin, just remember to

enjoy yourself – keep smiling and being the lovely friendly guy you really are.

How to Start a Conversation with a Woman

Girl Talk
The Right Approach

Girl 1: *Dan did it all right at the party. He wasn't focusing too much on me and being too obvious. He was engaging, but I didn't feel too homed in on. It was a good way of getting me interested.*

Girl 2: *I can't deal with that approach, because I never know whether they like me and I'm drunk and have written them off by the time I've realized they're into me. Someone has to be really direct with me or I just don't get it. They have to grab me and kiss me or ask me out for a drink or it's over my head.*

Now this is the problem – and also the wondrous thing – about the female of the species: girls come in all varieties. It's difficult to know until you try which approach is going to work. The most sensible – and successful – route to take when you're chatting up a girl is the one you feel most comfortable with. If you're honest (at least in the style of your approach), you won't seem like a charlatan and she'll be more likely to take a shine to you. But put an act on, and you'll put her off.

Square One – Requesting Sex

In 1995, the University of Arizona published the results of research they had carried out using 1,700 people. They had simply asked them how they would react to a request to have sex from a member of the opposite sex.

- Less than one per cent of women were flattered.
- Fifty per cent of women were insulted.
- Thirteen per cent of men were flattered.
- Eight per cent of men were insulted.

Are you one of the huge number of men that assumes men and women operate using the same model? Do you think we're all singing from the same hymn sheet? Ever wondered why compliments don't work when you judge a woman using your own value system? It's good to be 'well stacked' or have a 'great arse' after all, isn't it?

Goddamn, we've got work to do.

Instead of bulldozing straight in with the straightforward but artless, 'I fancy you, fancy a shag?', skirt around the issue at the forefront of your mind. You stand much more chance of getting under her skirt if you do. Here are a few general tips that'll help:

- Begin with something that doesn't put the focus – and hence the pressure – on the two of you. And don't make it something really poisonous about someone else, because no one likes a bitch.
- If you've opted for a chat-up line you've used before, don't make it too polished a delivery (that's not to say, develop a speech impediment). Neil Strauss's book *The Game* advises: 'Make your approach seem new, however

many times you've used it before.' Wise words.

- Perhaps ask for her help – not in a 'I-can't-seem-to-get-laid' way, but in a 'Where-might-I-get-cigarettes-at-this-time-of-night?' way. This achieves a double strike: most people love to help; you'll mark yourself out as the fresh, exotic, new kid in town. Everybody loves the new one – and she'll want first dibs.

- The apparently accidental, premature 'we' can work wonders. Make sure it relates to the two of you in the here and now though: 'What do you think they'd do if we started trashing the place?'

- Keep it casual, assured, throwaway, smiley. Don't be too direct or confrontational.

- Don't worry too much about what you say. Trying too hard is the quickest route to nowhere at all.

- Try not to talk too much. Use a trick that interviewers use – leave a pause after she's finished answering your question. She'll probably try to fill the silence and then you've got a conversation situation. Make sure you listen to what she's saying.

- Rid yourself of the idea of failure. All this is a learning experience. Stop caring so darned much. If she's not biting, move on to the next one. Plenty more fish in the sea.

- And finally, don't leave her with *nothing* to say back to you. A friend of a friend was once a chalet maid for a bunch of Welsh rugby players. One night after a good meal and plenty of wine, she was getting on particularly well with one of them. There was some chatting, a little flirting and then he felt his moment had come. 'I've got some talc in my room,' he said.

'Mrs Robinson, if you don't mind me saying so, this conversation is getting a little strange.'
– Benjamin (Dustin Hoffman) in *The Graduate* (1967)

How to Give a Compliment

What an art this is, but how important if you want to get laid.

Timing

Don't blunder straight in with a compliment – it might sound like a cheesy line. The killer compliment appears at least to have grown out of your conversation or the experience you're sharing. Throw in something like 'You're perceptive, aren't you?' after some observation on her part, and she's half won.

Substance

If you compliment her too quickly, all you'll be able to do is remark on some aspect of her appearance, which only works for some girls, and almost none if it's centred on her breasts/bum/legs, however awestruck you are by them. Beware the cliché, too: 'You've got lovely eyes' has been done to death. Be the exception to the rule, rather than wheeling out the same old chestnuts time and time again. Try to stand out – be different, insightful, unusual in what you find attractive about her. But get the balance right: compliment her on the sensitive part just behind her ear the first time you lay eyes on her, and she'll just think you're odd.

Style
Compliments should not be delivered too numerously or in an oily way. They must be dropped in as if you were musing on her briefly. Then a smile and move on, however much she wants to stay there, basking in your praise. Make her wait for another, and she'll strive to get them.

Over to Her
Of course, there are no guarantees about how she will receive your carefully selected offering. If she's a lady, she'll say a composed, 'Thank you.' If she's a bitch, she'll throw it back in your face. But if she's like most of us, she'll disagree with you in some flustered and hopefully quite charming way.

FINE LINES
When giving someone you've just met an unexpectedly lingering kiss on the lips as you leave for another appointment: 'I'd like to do more of that.'

The Art of Conversation
Make sure you use the chat-up conversation to your advantage: make it part of your foreplay. If you can get a girl hanging on to your every word, she'll be hanging on to the headboard before you know it.

Often, the key to seducing a lady is to make her feel like the most interesting, amazing person you've ever met. To do this, keep the focus on her. If she asks you a question, answer it, but then turn the spotlight back on her. It shouldn't feel like an interrogation, more like she's the most fascinating creature you've ever come across.

Another thing girls love is the idea of fate. She still buys into the idea that every girl has a Mr Right. She'll be a hundred times more likely to sleep with you if she thinks you're him (though beware the girls who prize potential relationships over one-night stands: they think that holding out means holding on to a man – she'll sleep with you only once the engagement ring is firmly on her finger). How to achieve this destined-to-be feel to your fling?

- Mirror her body language: cross your legs when she crosses hers; put an arm up on the back of your chair if she's done the same; copy the way her body moves when she laughs.
- Discover shared interests. She'll warm to you once she realizes you too are a closet karaoke fan.
- Come across amazing coincidences in your lives that shout (to a girl) that the pair of you were destined to meet. Perhaps you went to the same school or university; or your cousin knows her sister; or you both went on French camping holidays when you were young.
- Lead your witness. If she reveals anything you can latch on to, take the bait and follow it up with an agreement. Be it a political view or a pastime, if you share it she'll think you're soulmates. (NB: Follow this angle only if you're not a fan of the 'opposites attract' school of thought, for which you should disagree with everything she says, rousing both her temper and her temperature, resulting in a passionate thrashing out of your divergent opinions in the sack.)

This may all sound like a piece of piss. But be warned: lying will only get you so far. Profess an enthusiastic but fake interest in astrophysics and you'll soon be struggling. Even if you manage to seduce her on false terms, you won't be able to continue the fling. 'Who cares?' you might say. And in some cases, that's the best outcome. But what if she turns out to be the most incredible shag ever? (Sorry, ahem, 'person'.) Then you'll be sorry. So it's best to be straight. I'd never, ever recommend lying to get a girl into bed. Even if the falsehood works a treat, you run the risk of being found out before you've had your way with her, making all the groundwork a waste of time. Be straight, and your success rate will reflect it.

Pulling Your Partner

Moving in for the kill should never stop – even after you've captured your prey time and time again. Keep flirting with and attempting to seduce your partner. Always. Don't make it a rare occurrence like Candy's boyfriend: 'I can tell when my partner wants to get laid because he starts listening to me,' she says. 'Usually when I talk, he says it's just like white noise. He zones out completely. If he wants sex, he starts asking me stuff.'

Keep up the passionate pressure with the following:
• Send flirty text messages telling her what you'd like to do to her. (If you've never sent a filthy text, you're misusing the communication medium.)
• Buy her a very posh pair of knickers and suggest that they might become her pulling pants. Tell her

if she wears them, it's a signal to you that she wants it that day or night.

- Talk dirty to her – it always perks things up.
- The normal rules apply: listen, be interested.
- Maintain the element of surprise.
- Book trips away – as everyone knows, it's better on holiday.
- If you've got children, get a babysitter when there's no clear plan – it'll allow spontaneity.

Chat-Up 'Do's and 'Don't's

Do:

- Hold her hand a little longer than necessary when you first shake hands with her and employ that smile again. Just for her.
- Tell her she smells nice, but not in a *Silence-of-the-Lambs* way.
- Act naturally – that way you can't trip yourself up.
- Concentrate entirely on her. There are plenty more fish in the sea, but you can reel them in only one at a time. No looking over her shoulder at other fit women; no zoning out her chatter because you're finding her dull.

FINE LINES

A no-frills one this – but effective if delivered simply rather than lecherously: 'I like you. I'd like to spend the night with you.'

Don't:

- Do all the talking. It's boring and, more crucially, people will tell you all you need to know about them within five minutes of meeting them if you listen. Keep an air of mystery about you instead.

- Paw her. Keep to conversation when you're starting your seduction. The occasional, barely-there touch on her knee, back or arm is acceptable, but anything more and she'll just think you're sleazy. Hold back now and there'll be no holding back later.
- Talk about your future together as you start to bond. A degree of uncertainty is necessary for adventure and eroticism, as Joe found out:

Case Study: Joe

'It was the opening-night party for an erotica shop. I wasn't going to go home without pulling a girl on an occasion like that. Between the changing rooms there was a peephole and this babe stripped down to her underwear for me as I watched. We knew we were going home together then. We kissed passionately in the taxi all the way home – it was fantastic. Then, drunk and getting it on in my room, I stupidly said, "Let's go to Seville!" I was caught up in the moment. She grew cool straight away, made her excuses and left.'

A Shyness Clinic

Perhaps the reason you've not been getting laid has nothing to do with your chat-up technique, however. Maybe you're so shy you don't even have one. Have you been reading this book, thinking, 'Okay, I know I'm supposed to have a "confident, relaxed attitude", but I can't imagine ever being in that place?' Well, don't worry. Seriously, don't worry. The more you panic about these seductive situations, the worse your nerves are going to be. The reassuring thing is, women quite like shy guys. They think it shows a sensitive side, so you're already scoring points from the lairy lads who dominate the pick-up joints. It doesn't matter that you're just as keen to get her into bed as they are – she doesn't think that. She thinks she's special, the one person you've trusted to show your inner self to. Your shyness has given her the opportunity to feel caring, considerate: she's given you a chance when others might not have. Women love this – so you can turn your shyness to your advantage.

If talking to women makes you clam up entirely, though, it helps to learn a few tips to relax. Don't lose your unique charm, but at least these pointers will get you past 'hello':

1 Don't try to hide your shyness – or you'll tie yourself in knots of self-consciousness and have a terrible evening or, worst of all, come across as loud and arrogant, and give everyone else a terrible evening. As long as you tell people in a neutral, non-self-pitying way that you're shy, the vast majority will be sympathetic – because the vast majority are shy in certain circumstances. Don't make them feel like it's up to them to carry the conversation, but rather that you've shared a confidence with them. Shyness has a seductive element all its own.

With girls: make sure you don't cover up your shyness with apparent conceitedness.

2 Do as you would be done by socially – learn to listen. If you develop a genuine interest in other people and

99

what they have to say, making them feel comfortable and fascinating, they will do the rest for you. A simple but effective route to never being forgotten is to remember what was occupying the other person's mind for next time. Almost nobody does this and those that do will assume mythical status for the person remembered.

With girls: listen and remember stuff; question them; make them feel fascinating.

3 Have topics of conversation. It stands to reason that great conversationalists don't just blunder in, they prepare. They don't leave home without a handful of things to talk about, preferably tailored to the company they are about to keep. They remain abreast of current affairs. It's so obvious, but it works. Do this, and you'll tackle the twin problems of the shy person: you can avoid overcompensating and boring people by beginning too many sentences with 'I', and you can steer the conversation away from yourself.

With girls: Don't start too many sentences with 'I' or she'll be asleep long before you get your leg over; if you must tell stories, be sure they're entertaining ones.

4 Get out more and practise. Never turn down an invitation to go out. You never know who you might meet; even if you don't meet anyone, you're sharpening your arrows for the next time, when the sexiest woman in the room has caught your eye and is wandering over in your direction ...

When Girls are on the Pull

Speaking of which, sometimes – shy guy or no – you won't have to lift a finger to get laid. Sometimes she'll do all the work for you. Ah, that heavenly scenario for guys: when girls are on the pull.

Now, if this is the case, all you guys have to do is be picked up. Drag it out a little, even – it will titillate the seductress. The thrill is in the chase. Play it coy, but don't play too hard to get: the hot cookie sitting on your lap will just move on to someone else if she gets bored and doesn't scent success. If you can play your cards right, though, she'll have her hand on your inner thigh just to ask the time and her hand on your cock mere hours later. The best seductions happen when the woman seduces you. Though this book is packed with advice to turn you into a legendary ladykiller, sometimes all you have to do is follow her lead.

How to Spot When a Girl is on the Prowl

• **She's out with her lady friends, but she isn't 'hanging out' with them.** She won't be as giggly and girly as the rest of her pals, especially if the (often hilarious) subject of men comes up. The other girls are playing the role of her wingman. Sometimes the female wingman is obvious: women will employ a classic twosome approach much like the male one. On other occasions, there'll be a whole harem out for the night, but they simply provide an innocuous backdrop to the main action of one girl getting her end away.

• **She's casing the joint.** A female on the prowl seems more observant than her fellows: she's always keeping an eye out for a potential pull.

• **Individual sexy dancing.** She might be cavorting with her mates on the dance floor, but this lady isn't caught up

101

in the moment. She's well aware of what she's doing. Watch her eyes: she'll be looking for someone. Watch her body: she'll be twisting and turning in a way that's engineered to drive you wild.

• **Eye contact.** When she makes her move (or gives you all the signals so that you make yours), she'll hold eye contact with you for as long as possible during your dialogue, usually looking up at you from underneath her eyelashes (think of Diana, Princess of Wales, in that *Panorama* interview) and with a sexy little smile playing on her lips.

• **Laugh a minute.** She'll want you to think she's great fun. So she'll always be smiling and laughing – even when you're not being that funny.

• **Flying solo.** Her mates leave – but she stays to see out the night with you.

• **Touchy-feely.** She'll be all over you. Any opportunity to touch you she'll grab with both hands: thus you'll find her laying her palms flat on your chest; fondling your thighs; squeezing your arms and hands; stroking the back of your neck. She'll lean in close to speak to you, even if you can hear her perfectly well when she's sitting upright.

• **Her opening line is, 'Fancy a shag?'**

Case Study: Brian

'I was out one night for a few beers when I noticed that this girl kept looking over at me. I didn't think much of it, until she detached herself from her gang of mates and approached me. She asked me for a light: when she leaned forward to take it, she looked me deep in the eye like she was taking something else. I could see right down her top too. So there she was, puffing on her fag, blowing out the smoke in a really sexy way. We just started chatting. She was leading it all, though by now of course I knew what she was up to. I offered to buy her a drink and she accepted, even though her mates all decided to leave at that point. They were all laughing as they left, but she just smiled at me in this really lazy, lovely way. My mates left not long after. Eventually, so did we: together.'

How to Listen

Men think women talk too much; women think men don't listen. If you can distinguish yourself as Listener Man, you will already be an exotic breed apart – so listen carefully, because here are some tips that will really up your chances.

MRI scans show that men are not natural speakers. The whole of the left hemisphere of a man's brain is employed in finding a centre for speech when he is talking. A woman does it more easily, and it is centred around very specific areas on both sides of her brain. This leaves the rest of women's brains free to do other things.

Looking Like You're Listening

When you were a caveman, your expressionless demeanour paid dividends – but if you want to be a caveman with her, it'll help if you drop that mask. Women have evolved a range of listening expressions, which most men haven't. Watch women and learn from them. You'll be amazed at the results. In conversation, a woman uses about six expressions per ten seconds to show the person opposite her that she is listening not only to the words they're saying, but also to their body language and intonation. Carefully observe the way women work and then copy them mercilessly.

Tips for the conversation itself:

- Speak in low tones – squeaky tones don't become a man or a woman.
- Don't gabble – however nervous you feel and however much you have to say.
- Listen – and engage in what she's saying.
- Be friendly – although this is the last on the list, it is perhaps the most potent weapon in the pick-up artist's armoury. And the easiest to achieve.

What's That Sound? The Sound of a Man Ruining His Chances

It was all going so well. Your eyes had met across the room. There was a spark. Cigarette safely lit, you schmoozed across ... and got a slap in the face for your troubles. Perhaps you tried one of the following lines? Dear, oh dear. Guys, avoid these chat-up lines like the plague:

- 'Have you got a mirror in your pants? 'Cause I can see my face in them.'
- 'You remind me of a carpet – I can see you on my bedroom floor.'
- 'Would you like to come back to mine? I know Mum would love to meet you.'
- 'Want to go halves on a bastard?'
- 'You're almost as sexy as the last bird I pulled.'
- 'You're almost as sexy as your best friend.'
- 'I'm glad I met you now – I went to the clap clinic a couple of weeks ago and my STD has completely cleared up.'

And *please* tell me you didn't:

- Tell her her ranking, viz: 'There are quite a few half-decent girls here tonight – lots of 7s like you.'
- Ask to borrow money, so 'you' can 'buy' her a drink.

Finally, if any of the following apply, it's best to keep quiet about them:

- You're still in love with your ex and would drop everything and anybody if she clicked her fingers.
- You subscribe to a lads' mag (we might guess that you're rather fond of the *FHM* Hot 100 year on year, but we do not need to know about your archived collection – established 1989).
- When you see her, you can think only about shagging her.
- You slept with someone else last night.
- You hate condoms.
- You're obsessed with anal sex (boring).
- You don't like gays/foreigners/children/women.
- You don't like dogs/her dog/cats/her cat.
- In fact, you don't like or value anything.
- Including your own life.
- Less still hers.
- You're a bit of a moaner.
- You think most people are jerks.
- You think you're a bit of a catch.
- You have lucky pulling pants.

Body Language: All's Well That Ends Well

Assuming you haven't blown it, if once you're talking to her she does more than one of the following, you are well in there, my friend:

- Her feet are pointing towards you – this is a good sign. You are the direction she's headed in.
- She's finding excuses to touch you – but guys, it should be said that women do this for increased intimacy in general, whether it be with a man or a woman. It's not necessarily a come-on (although she obviously doesn't find you repulsive, so build on that).
- She mirrors your movements: you're on the same wavelength.
- She keeps looking at your mouth – she's thinking about being kissed by it.
- She keeps crossing and uncrossing her legs – she's drawing attention to them, and what they lead up to ...

Top Ten Signs She Wants You

10 She's giving her glass a hand job.

9 She's checking herself in the mirror when you go to the bar or on her way back from the loo.

8 She's taking drags of your cigarette.

7 She's asking you to check her skirt's not got twisted at the back – while deliberately giving you an eyeful of her arse.

6 She's sitting on your lap and you only met her that night.

5 She's touching her mouth a *lot*, drawing your attention to it and occasionally slipping her finger inside.

4   She's going through your wallet – in a nice way –
    laughing at the funny picture on your gym card
    and asking questions about what she finds there
    (hopefully not 'Why haven't you got any money?').
3   She's resisting the approaches of other men.
2   She's letting her friends go home without her.
1   She's simulating sex with you on the dance floor.

||||| ||
Playing with Your Prey

Well, that went well. She's interested. She may be so interested that you've taken her straight home and are just about ready for the evening's main event. In which case, what are you doing here? Sidestep this chapter and head straight for 'Consuming Your Prey' – see page 131. For the rest of you, don't be disheartened. You're not always going to get laid just by meeting a girl and instantly hitting it off – usually, and more and more frequently as you get older, you're going to have to put in some time and effort before you reap the rewards. Which means dating. Don't think of this as a drag, think of it as the delicious starter before the main course. This is where it gets interesting. Knock her socks off with some well-designed dates and she'll be even more willing when the two of you eventually get it on.

Before the key question of where to take her crops up, however, you have to set up the rendezvous in the first place. Don't be too short-term in your strategy when you're arranging your date. Here's what not to do:

Case Study: Matt

'I met Matt in a swanky cocktail bar one night. He was so attentive towards me it was almost off-putting. But he was quite a sweet, entertaining bloke and this was fun, so I gave him my number. Soon after, the texting started. We exchanged several texts a day, just a bit of banter and a few "Morning, Beautiful" ones from him. He sent me flowers to the office – nice touch – and we arranged to meet up. The day of the date arrived and he called in the morning to say he couldn't wait to see me again, but at 7 p.m. I got a text from him: he couldn't make it because his car had broken down. Could he postpone? I said yes, but I already knew I'd never hear from him again. I just don't get it. Why do guys put in all that initial effort, only to back out at the last minute? Have the balls actually to date girls you chat up, or you're all mouth and no nookie – and what's the point in that?'

Another pitfall when arranging a date: don't impose a dress code on her purely for your own satisfaction – e.g. 'You can wear your best shoes' – because she'll feel railroaded and typecast ('Oh, can I now?'). I've thought twice when men have offered me this attractive option. In my world, you have to earn me dressing up for you.

Case Study: Edward

'Ed the lawyer got it right. He made me dressing up an integral part of the adventure. "I'm taking you to a club in St James's and then an old-school wine bar on Fleet Street," he said. "Should be fun. These places aren't going to be around much longer. Only thing is, you have to wear a skirt, I'm afraid." Needless to say, he had me girling up in a heartbeat

Top Ten Ways to Sweep Her Off Her Feet

If you really want to make a good impression, any of
the following will make her moist before you've even
kissed her:

10 Opening her car door.

9 Putting your coat over her shoulders if it's cold.

8 Sending over a fancy cocktail.

7 Remembering details – what she was doing last
night; her friends' names; that she's a vegetarian,
and so on.

6 Arranging for champagne to be chilling on ice.

5 Test-driving a Ferrari and taking her for a spin
(but remember she'll be less impressed by the car
than you are, so keep a lid on those rapturous
speeches about how she does 0-60 in 2.8 seconds
and handles like a dream).

4 Giving her roses (pre-bought and wrapped, not
the single-stem variety hawked by dodgy-looking
geezers in nightclubs).

3 Quoting poetry (take the time to look some up next time you're in the library picking up girls). Best of all, writing your own poem or song about her and then giving an impromptu performance.

2 Taking her on a hot-air balloon ride – you're quite literally sweeping her off her feet.

1 Finding out what her favourite food is and then cooking it for her.

This last pointer is an absolute sure-fire hit. I should know – we women use it all the time on you men, after all. It's even more effective when the roles are reversed. Cooking for her involves:

- Making an effort (you're not just in it for the short-term, she thinks).
- Her having to be appreciative of you (to be expressed in a physical fashion, you can only hope).
- Having her round to your place (where there is no escape ...).

Before you start stocking up on condoms, however, give a bit of thought as to whether your home is the seductive setting it needs to be. While buying candles for the dinner table (or at least soft lights for the living room) will contribute to the amorous atmosphere, you'll need to do a full sweep of the entire apartment before it's safe to let her cross the threshold. Whether you live in a palace or a bachelor pad, there are some basics that you should bear in mind:

- Put away childish things – clear away signs that you live off pre-packaged food and takeaways, and that all you ever do is play PS2.

- Stash the porn/lads' mags.
- Get rid of telltale hair conditioner/high heels/sex toys from your previous – or current on/off – relationship.
- Avoid a relentlessly male apartment – i.e. one that looks like the kitchen has been visited only to light cigarettes off the gas or from the toaster.
- Nor should your flat be too 'designed'. It should look like you've given it a bit of thought – a nice sofa, for instance – but not like you got your gay mate to design it for you. That would be not only intimidating for the average girl, but creepy and confusing.
- Give the bathroom a quick clean. It doesn't have to be sparkling, but at least squirt some bleach in the loo and scrub away dodgy stains.
- Don't put on an act. It's your home, after all: you should be at your most relaxed there. (It should go without saying: be relaxed, but don't forget the company. She won't be impressed if you fart all over the place shouting, 'Fruity!') Don't try to 'stage' things either – it feels false. Peter was rumbled when he tried this out:

Case Study: Peter

'I'd arranged for a lady friend to come round for dinner one night. I was very well organized, if I say so myself: very expensive, carefully considered wine chilling in the fridge; dinner simmering on the stove; the place cleaned and cleared and ready for action. But there was something missing. I'm a graphic designer, so I thought it would be a great idea to be sketching when she arrived – just casually getting on with my work, but obviously showcasing my creative, talented side at the same time. I thought she'd be knocked for six. So when the doorbell went, I had my sketch pad out and was midway through a company logo. I left her in the sitting room with the artwork as I went to fetch our drinks. As I'd planned, she scooted over to the sketch pad as soon as I left the room. But what happened next was quite unexpected: I heard her snickering. Snickering. She was obviously fighting back the giggles as I came back in. My advice would be never to pose ostentatiously: it always backfires.'

Dinner at Eight

If you're brave enough to go the whole hog and properly cook for her (as opposed to buying top-class ready meals), *keep it simple*. Even if you pull off something extravagant, you're likely to be so distracted that she'll think you've gone off her. And watch your alcohol intake when cooking. It's fine for the food to be well marinated – the same doesn't go for the host.

Case Study: Dom

'A guy called Dom once slow-cooked a pork belly for me on a dinner date we had round at his. But by the time it was ready, he was so drunk he couldn't even be bothered to carve it – he handed the carving knife to me. There were no more assignations after that, as you can imagine. In fact, he's lucky I didn't use the bloody thing on him.'

A few further words of advice:

- Simplicity is key (I can't stress this enough).
- Set the scene – really make an effort for her. Lay the table in advance, buy some napkins, light some candles and soften the mood.
- It doesn't matter if it goes wrong – don't panic or throw her out if there is some culinary disaster. She may be able to help (in which case, she'll enjoy the feeling of being a domestic goddess: this could play out well for you); if she can't, there's always the pizza delivery service and a memorable date that both of you can smile about later.
- Remember that eating with your fingers is incredibly sensual. Feeding each other is pretty sexy too. For dessert, lay on some strawberries, perhaps with a small bowl of melted chocolate to dip them into. The lips and mouth are two very responsive erogenous zones (see page 141): get her appreciating their sexual potential before you've retired to the bedroom and she'll be hotting up just sitting across from you at the dinner table.

Aphrodisiac Foods

Of course, you should give consideration to what you're going to cook for her too. There is a potent and under-explored relationship between food and arousal. Some foods look rude (oysters, figs), some release happy hormones and some increase blood flow – including blood flow to your sexual organs (that'll be ginger). Oysters also release D-aspartic acid and NMDA, which stimulate the release of the hormones testosterone and oestrogen. But whatever the science, all you really need to know is that certain foods will get her feeling frisky – so it's well worth adding them to the menu.

The relationship between other foods and sex is less direct, but just as relevant. Bananas, for instance: as well as being a rude shape, they are meant to raise self-confidence and lift the brain's mood – both to be encouraged in a sexual partner. Banana fritters, anyone? A guy I was dating once got a hard-on watching me eat banana fritters, which is why they come to mind.

Also try including some of the following in your repertoire:
- **Avocado** – the Aztecs swore by it as an aphrodisiac, because it's full of nutritional goodness and shaped a bit like a lady and a bit like a lady's bits.
- **Apple** – round, juicy and associated with temptation for over two thousand years.
- **Asparagus** – as well as looking like a mucky little chap, it's rich in good things for energy levels and hormone production: calcium, phosphorous, potassium.
- **Chocolate** – gives energy and it also contains a substance similar to a happy hormone.
- **Cucumber** – the smell alone increases blood flow to the vagina, so she'll be slick without you having to lift a finger.

- **Garlic** – according to the Romans it increased virility and fertility. Contrary to the stereotype, no one sexy minds the breath it gives you.
- **Carrots** – may not make you see in the dark, but these phallic fellows will certainly improve your nocturnal abilities all the same. Thought to be more of a male stimulant, so watch out for unexpected arousal.
- **Olives** – green ones make men more virile; black boost a woman's sex drive.
- **Pine nuts** – felt by those in the know to have magical effects as an aphrodisiac.
- **Seafood** – especially oysters.

Also sexy for women are mangos, yams and green peas – though not necessarily at the same time. Beware of cherries and roasting meat. These are meant to inhibit sexual desire in women.

Scents and Sensuality

'Oh, for a Life of Sensations rather than of Thoughts!'
– John Keats

Having explored aphrodisiac foods, you may be interested to learn about another key sensual element in the art of seduction: aromatherapy. Yes, okay, it sounds totally girly, but it could get you girl action, so it's worth paying attention. However base and straightforward your instincts may be, to be sure of getting laid, you're going to have to appeal to all of her senses. Having seduced her through her lips, mouth and tongue, now employ her nostrils in your noble nookie quest.

Aromas can be transmitted around your home by burning oil or incense sticks. If you don't go in for that kind of stuff, you can burn candles, use a room or linen spray or, as a last resort, wear them. And if your hackles are going up at the thought of buying a 'room or linen spray' (something I'm sure you never thought would make an appearance on your shopping list), consider the intended end result ... and you're back in the room. At least one or two of the following are bound to get her going (but don't use them all at once):

- **Jasmine**: a magical, night-time aroma. Put it in oil or incense, or spray your bedlinen with the slightest hint of it.

- **Ylang-ylang**: this is a more blatant scent, gorgeous but not to every girl's taste. Is she slightly outrageous and already pretty up for it? You're probably all right, then.

- **Rose**, especially Rose Otto: when she wants to drift off to another place, she puts this in her bath. If there's a hint of it around you or your place, she'll think you're a class act.

- **Musk**: a cliché perhaps, but it makes us women wild because its smell resembles the male pheromone. Yum. Wear the tiniest bit of oil on a pulse point or two. Go on, I dare you.

- **Vanilla**: a sexy, sweet but sophisticated smell that's supposed to do it for both men and women. Maybe we just remind each other of ice cream when we wear it.

- **Patchouli**: thought to have aphrodisiac qualities, but I think this is a risky one. Use only on the out-and-out hippy chick.

- **Peppermint**: stimulating rather than erotic. Perhaps worth a try if things are getting a bit languid for your liking and you want to wake her up a bit. Watch out though – she might just wake up, get her coat and leave.

- **Lemon or orange citrus** – and bergamot too. Like vanilla and musk, good ingredients for a man's cologne.

- **Sandalwood:** a popular 'note' in men's aftershave that is supposed to stimulate part of the nervous system. I don't like it, but many do.
- **Lavender:** to you it says 'old ladies', to her it says 'powerful sexual stimulant'. Is it worth having to overcome the associations with the first on the off-chance that the second is true? Your call.

The Wider World

If your cooking skills aren't up to much, or if you're still not sure she'll agree to visit your humble home (girls aren't stupid: we know once we're there it'll be harder to turn you down), then you'll have to date her in the wider world. Here's Rachel's view:

Case Study: Rachel

'Cinema then a meal is brilliant for a date, though not for the first few as you can't talk to each other at the movies. On one date I went to see *In the Cut*, which is possibly the most erotic film I've ever seen. It was a bit weird sitting next to this person and watching something like that, but it gave us something to talk about afterwards in a slightly giggly and awkward way. In case we'd been wondering, it was obvious that there was sexual tension between us after that.'

The cinema is certainly a popular choice for a date location – perhaps because of the darkened atmosphere, which persuades many to lose their inhibitions ...

Pulling Your Partner

Case Study: Barry and Jill

Barry and Jill have mastered the art of keeping it alive. Whenever they go to the cinema, there is always a race to get to the bottom of their family-size sweet-'n'-salty popcorn carton. Why? Are they so bored by each other that they have to gorge themselves to compensate for it? Not a bit of it. Once they've finished the popcorn, they pop out the bottom of the carton and she gives him a well-disguised hand job.

At the Table

Taking a girl out for dinner is a traditional but still popular date. You might think it would be pretty straightforward to wine and dine a lady into bed – but there are some pitfalls to avoid. First up: table manners. Remember:

- Use cutlery from the outside in – not as confusing as it's made out to be: the little knives and forks deal with the little courses.
- Tear bread rolls in half, don't cut them – not applicable to other foodstuffs. Like fish, for instance, or potatoes.
- Don't drink straight from your soup bowl – and tilt it and your spoon away from you to get the last bits out of the bottom.

Consider the conversation you're having, too. Think back to 'Moving in for the Kill', when you studied the art of conversation – just because this is the second or third time you've met her, it doesn't mean you should treat her any differently. In fact, she's here *because* of the way you treated her, so keep up the good work. Try to recall what you talked about the last time – don't go over old ground, but revisit what she was interested in. She'll be thrilled that you remembered.

Pulling Your Partner

There's no reason to stop dating your girlfriend just because you've got together. Keep things playful between the two of you. Keep making time for each other. This isn't as hard as it sounds. Turn the television off once in a while – you don't need as much energy as you think for sex. And you don't need to be on the pull to take her out.

Case Study: Phil and Jo

These two are clear on how they've managed to stay together all these years. 'Once a week, on a Wednesday, we go to a little bistro round the corner,' says Phil. 'It's written in stone. Nothing – barring illness or a holiday – can move it. And when we're there, we talk.'

Talking Too Much

Certain types of men constantly need reminding not to talk too much on a first date and, in general, this can just about be forgiven. Perhaps he's a bit nervous, we think. Perhaps his parents led him to believe he was responsible for carrying an evening out with a girl. Combine this with showing off and being overbearing, though, and unless you're on a date with a slug, you're done for. Don't hijack the conversational territory, as Brad did to his detriment:

Case Study: Brad

Sarah went on a blind date with Brad, a man who couldn't stop talking about his exciting achievements and his unfailing ability to suck the marrow out of life. It was blah blah skydiving this; blah blah Great Barrier Reef that; blah blah rip curl the other. His chances of getting laid were slipping away like the ground beneath his feet in the desert he once visited in the middle of a sandstorm.

And then the pièce de résistance. After an hour or so of leading this joyous celebration of his own life, as Sarah sat by, quietly drowning in the white water of his self-obsession, our hero remembered his manners. 'What about you?' he said. (A faint glimmer of hope stirred in her heart.) 'What exciting things have you done?'

Panic. 'Um ...' 'Think,' she thought, 'think.' But nothing. She may have done some exciting things, but by then she had no idea of them. Brad had hijacked the conversational territory and left Sarah with no role but to sit there, dumb and stunned – and not in a good way.

Are You a Bore?
'Beware the conversationalist who adds "in other words". He is merely starting afresh.'
– Robert Morley

If you're worried your personality might be letting you down in the sex stakes, it's a great big 'yes' if you:

- Notice girls rubbing their cheeks and blinking rapidly as they move away from you, such is the pain they're feeling from holding that glazed, smiling expression for so long.
- Notice people wandering off just when you're getting to the good bit.
- Spot a rugby scrum to sit as far away from you as possible at the dinner table.
- Clock girls looking terrified instead of answering your query at the appropriate time. They've no idea what you asked them! They've been thinking about other things for the past half-hour!
- Realize people are making absurd excuses to mingle.

The problem is, of course, that if you're a true bore you won't notice any of the above or anything else very much. And no one will tell you you're a bore, so you'll continue to bore on in blissful ignorance till the end of your days. Have I given you the fear yet? Good! There's a bit of a bore in every man (and many women, come to that) – be on your guard for it at all times and make immediate amends whenever you notice your conversations taking a turn for the worse.

Are You a Psycho?
Let's hope not. Scaring girls off and don't know why? The key thing is not to be too full-on with women – be it

texting or calling them all the time ... or suggesting you lock them up in your Dungeon of Power on a first date.

Case Study: Amanda

'I got chatted up at a theme park by this American guy. He was thirty and there with his parents, so I should have realized that something was amiss. As it was, I went out with him for a year. But there was one, rather significant problem. For Valentine's Day that year, he made me a card, all by himself (aah). It was a big piece of card with a heart on it. What's that, you say? Drawn on with a coloured pencil? No, fashioned out of bullet holes, actually. He had shot me a Valentine's card.'

There's a message here, guys: you may think your prowess with a huge weapon will delight her – it's more likely to have her dialling 999 at the earliest opportunity.

How to Get Laid on a First Date

'A little still she strove, and much repented,
And whispering "I will ne'er consent" – consented.'
– Lord Byron, *Don Juan*

The trick for no-tears first-date shagging is to make it seem like the most fun option available to both of you by the end of the night. Even if it's been your aim from the outset, give the other person the impression that it's a conclusion you've arrived at together during the course of the evening.

Women are more and more up for casual sex, but you're unlikely to take her to heaven and back during a one-off and she knows this, so it must seem like the perfect end to the night's adventure. The night, then, must be an adventure. According to Neil Strauss's *The Game*, 'it takes roughly seven hours for a woman to be comfortably led from meet to sex'. The clock's ticking ... Whisk her off to places she's never been before – don't think parties and pubs, but private drinking clubs and secret gardens. Give her the fantasy night she never thought she'd actually live out. Enchant her. Whoever thought the cinema was the place for a first date? Not only are you not able to talk to and charm each other, you're not even able to look at each other. Keep away!

You don't have to spend a lot of money, but give the impression that you know your patch. Offer her the best dim sum in town, or take her to the coolest little hip-hop joint or the place that mixes the perfect Martini. She'll be on all fours, eating out of your hand in no time – if that's your thing.

Another point worth bearing in mind about women is that – unlike you – they're suckers for being teased and for deferred gratification, so you need to be desired by her from the earliest possible point in the evening. Don't, whatever you do, be too cool. Don't listen to your 'you've-got-all-the-time-in-the-world' mate's advice. He hasn't got laid for ages. Instead, show her early on that you're keen – but don't shove it down her throat. It's not a one-way process and she needs to make up her mind about you. Remember those gentlemanly manners? (See page 86.) Employ them now. Make her feel classy, and she'll love the transition later in the evening when she shows you the other side of her personality – that of the dirty bitch.

FINE LINES

'I'm in no hurry.' (This is what you say to her, but obviously don't take yourself at your word, Mr 'Time Is On My Side'.)

'I'm in no hurry – cut to: sharing a post-coital cigarette,' as one guy who used this line on me once observed wryly over a post-coital cigarette. I'd laughed at his jokes, dithered about whether I was ready for what he might want from me ... but 'I'm in no hurry' was the line that sold going to bed with him to me. We're all suckers for a lack of obligation. Try it.

Top Ten Dates for Getting Laid

10 Tenpin bowling – or any activity which involves you getting behind her and 'helping' her with her stance. Anyone for golf?

9 The aquarium – especially if there are dolphins. All girls have a thing for dolphins. Take her to see some of them showing off their tricks and she'll be performing in your hands before you know it.

8 A night at the dogs. Adrenaline-charged atmosphere; packed with people risking things and taking a punt; full of old men, apart from you – what's not to like? Even glamorous girls will enjoy the perverse thrill of roughing it over scampi and chips and placing their bets with the waitress.

7 Swimming pool. You can see her nearly naked and show her your carefully rehearsed diving skills. And don't discount all that exercise with its feel-good endorphins ...

6 Clay-pigeon shooting. Opportunities for physical contact as you help her with her grip. Those guns give off a faint whiff of danger in the country air ... Plus, she'll think you're loaded, which is a bit of an aphrodisiac to some women.

5 Funfair. Scary or novel things – like riding a roller coaster – trigger dopamine to the brain, which gives her a flutter that feels like love. You'll find that she's flustered and excited – pink-cheeked, buzzing and up for going on all the rides, again and again and again (just what you like in a girl). Try not to be sick, and perhaps steer her away from the candyfloss and toffee apples beforehand so that she isn't either.

4 A room with a view. Find a place with a breathtaking spectacle the two of you can take in. Perhaps a bar at the top of a skyscraper; or take a cable car up to the top of a mountain; or escort her to a viewing of a total eclipse (planetary alignments permitting). Go for a daytime stroll and take in the panoramic vista of a local beauty spot. You'll be the one taking her breath away before too long.

3 Wine tasting. Achieves the double strike of making you seem cultivated and getting her trolleyed and up for anything at the same time.

2 A little restaurant you know. It ain't neuroscience. If you show her you know your patch and all its secret places like the back of your hand, subconsciously she'll receive the message that you'll probably be an expert on all her secret places too.

1 Rowing boat on a lake. This featured in *Bridget Jones's Diary*, so she'll be tingling with excitement before you've even set sail. Plus points: there's no escape; the gentle rocking motion of the boat will hopefully put her in mind of other rhythmic activities (NB: Not group percussion); throw in a bottle of champagne and you're away.

||||| |||
Consuming Your Prey

So, you've got your prey home, safe and sound, and you're just moments away from the bedroom. Hearty congratulations! But be warned: the deal is by no means sealed. She may have taken you at your word when you studied 'Fine Lines' and said, 'I'm in no hurry.' It may be that she's just realized she's locked out and needs a sofa to crash on. The sight of your bedroom alone may be enough to send her running for the hills, even if she was as keen as Dijon just moments before. To stop her from scarpering, a damage-limitation exercise is called for – and quickly. Help is at hand with this nifty guide:

Damage Limitation in the Home:

A Ten-Point Plan

1 Get her a drink while you quickly tidy your room. It is worth putting her down for a moment – she'll be out of there before you can say, 'Never done laundry in my life,' if she actually sees the state of your sheets.

2 Perhaps suggest she puts some music on (the time it takes her to choose a CD will prove invaluable). Mentally vet your record collection first, and remember your chat-up lines from earlier in the night. Lying wasn't advised (see page 96), but if you just happened

131

to mention off the cuff that you were a hot record producer, question now whether your CD rack will support such a bold claim.

3 Once in your room, make the bed.

4 Hide the worst of the damage. Any mouldy plates should be swiftly dispatched – even to the bin. You can always buy more plates – you have only one chance with this lady.

5 Open your windows – if it's not arctic temperatures outside. A girl who's goose-pimpled will not be keen to shed her clothes. (In fact, it might be an idea to whack up the central heating, just to encourage her to strip off.)

6 If you can't air the room and it smells (if in doubt, it does), blast some deodorant around.

7 Put your dirty laundry in the laundry bin (if you don't have one, the bottom of the wardrobe will do – just as long as she doesn't start looking for one of your shirts to wear, to do that cute-girl-wearing-nothing-but-a-man's-shirt thing).

8 You won't have time to change the sheets (though thank your Boy Scout 'be prepared' motto, or your healthy dose of arrogance, if you thought to do it before you went out), but you can buy linen spray for this very occasion. It will freshen up those stinky sheets, while – potentially – also turning her on (see page 117). Keep it out of sight though: the fragrance is seductive; the idea of you buying girly linen spray is not.

9 If there are any dodgy stains on your bed, your only option is to dim the lights. Light candles if you have any. Everything looks better in soft light.

10 Now you can rejoin her – and only hope she hasn't wandered into the kitchen in your absence.

Case Study: Jeremy

Jeremy had Molly back to his flat for the first time. It was a bit of a bachelor pad if he was honest: a bit uncared for, no pictures on the walls. Trying to find something to say, Molly noted, 'Oh look, you've got a nice big kitchen. I wish I had a big kitchen to cook in, I think it would make me cook all the time.' Seeing his chance, Jeremy chipped in, 'Well, you can always come over here and cook for me and my flatmate.'

Guys, if it's a mother you're after rather than a lover, try to conceal this, at least until after you've got laid. If you say the wrong thing, no matter how tidy your room is or even how dirty, she ain't gonna stick around.

Miracle Maneouvres to Get Things on to the Next Stage

You're side by side on the couch. She's come back with you, she's seen the state of the place and yet stayed, but the relaxed, flirty bubble the two of you were in at the party seems to have well and truly burst. You're nervous, you're impatient, you want to move things on, but how can you do it subtly, seductively and with a guarantee of success?

Well, don't do as a famous writer once did with me: sigh like you're a WWI soldier steeling yourself to go over the top of a trench, slam your Sea Breeze forcefully on the table and lay a hand on her knee. I didn't realize how nervous he was until then. I was staying anyway – it was too late to get a train and too far to get a cab – but all this did was convince me that he was going to be a clumsy and self-conscious lover.

Try one of the following smooth moves instead:

- **The shoulder brush.** If the conversation's going well, as you walk to the kitchen/mini-bar to replenish your glasses, brush her shoulder lightly and leave your hand there while you ask her what she'd like to drink. If she touches you back – or grabs you and kisses you full on the mouth – then she's interested.
- **Get her to touch you.** A move that must be carried off with considerable aplomb. If she's the flaky New Age type, perhaps get her into some conversation about reading palms or being able to measure the length of someone's feet by looking at the length of their forearm or something. Actually getting your feet out at this stage is risky (see page 30). If she's a normal gal, you could opt for the fail-safe 'I think I've got something in my eye – could you please take a look?' Cue her looking deep into your eyes, gently touching your face to angle the light on to it. Or get a crick in your neck. She's likely to volunteer to massage it: that always hits the spot.
- **Touch her for 'another reason'.** For example, to do her coat up because it's cold (only if you're outside, obviously); or put your hat on her or something cute like that. If you're really stylish, you'll touch her just once and leave it at that for the moment.
- **Massage – you on her.** If you can't turn a massage situation into a making-out situation, then there's no hope for you. From behind, touch her neck lightly with the tips of your fingers for a bit. Then brush it with your lips. Don't throw her on to her back and lunge at her –

leave that for on-screen Hollywood lovers. See also the foot massage, below. Seduce her from head to toe.

Erogenous Zones You Neglect, But Shouldn't

'This is a boy, sir. Not a girl. If you're baffled by the difference it might be as well to approach both with caution.'
– Match in *What the Butler Saw*, Joe Orton, 1969

Feet

Never underestimate the power of a good foot massage – and don't forget each individual toe and the tops of the feet as you go. Start off gently and increase the pressure. Ask her what feels good, because some people like firmer pressure than others and some are incredibly ticklish. Don't be absent-minded – she'll be taking an interest in your approach because she'll subconsciously think it's representative of your approach to sex. Speaking of which, the foot massage is an excellent transition to intercourse. One minute you might be watching TV, the next she's got her eyes closed and is en route to ecstasy.

Backs of Knees and Inner Thighs

Obvious places to proceed to after the foot massage. Take your time, however tempted you are to try and rush on into her. Don't forget she can still get up and go at any moment. Seduce her. Work your way up slowly, teasing as you go ... She'll be completely ready for you by the time you reach the top. Make her wait and you'll already have blown 99 per cent of the male opposition out of the water. She'll never forget you. She'll be yours for the taking whenever you choose.

Underside of Her Arms

As a pick-up artist once observed, with women the underside of everything is the most sensitive – including the breasts and buttocks. Before you get on to those main attractions, concentrate on her arms. Use the tips of your fingers and brush with your lips, but not too lightly, or it'll just be irritating and make her itch.

Neck

This is so hot, but somehow on your mission to get inside us, you often forget it. A bit of an oversight, really, because some well-targeted neck action is a direct route to being 'ready' for most girls. Use your lips and the tips of your fingers at the same time and – gently, gently – flicks of your tongue and the slightest pressure with your teeth and ... mmm.

Ears

Journey to here via her neck. Begin below and behind her ears and then start to nuzzle her ear lobes. Pull at them gently with your lips and your teeth. Beware of licking, which can be off-putting – of course it's loud for her, you're just by her ear! I think whispering sweet nothings or talking dirty at this point is hazardous. There are men who can get away with talking dirty on the first night, but you may not be one of them. There's only one way to find out, and if you get it wrong you'll have blown your chance to get laid. I'd avoid tongue action and talking if you don't know each other all that well: unless her moans and groans indicate that she's away with the fairies already, of course.

Hands

When the time feels right, plunge one of her fingers into your mouth and lick at it at the same time. A degree of disorientation works wonders with sex and this will remind her of what she'll do to you when you get inside her. The palms of the hands contain tens of thousands of nerve endings too, so bury your mouth in them and lick away, giving her a foretaste of what it'll feel like when you go down on her.

Once in bed, it's worth getting the sex right, if only so that she's more likely to say yes if you fancy going again.

Do:
- Do it with love, if only love for the opposite sex or for sex itself. Sometimes this is enough for both of you. It's the perfect end to the night's adventure. You are partners in crime.
- Tease in bed. Now and for ever. Amen.
- Know when to shut up. Humour probably got the two of you into bed in the first place, but hold it there. Nobody likes a chatty lover or bantering in bed.

Don't:
- Kiss with pursed lips like she's your granny. Do you want to be thinking about your granny right now? Well, then.
- Ask her what she wants too much. It'll feel like an exam. Nobody wants to be thinking in bed. Read about erogenous zones (see above and page 141) before you even go out and if you're still stuck for things to do, give choices: 'Which is better: this, or this?'
- Forget that women take time to warm up. A friend once told me: 'Men think in functional straight lines; women think in picturesque curves. That's all you need to know. Apply this to whatever you like: it's the same with journeys, sex, conversation, everything.' So while you're busy racing from A to B in sixty seconds, we prefer to

let our engines tick over for a little while, making sure we've got enough oil and water to stay the distance, and only then do we begin the excursion. Come with us – and don't forget the map.

Girl Talk

'If you want to know how to seduce a woman, watch Nine and a Half Weeks.*'*

Matters of Size

Does size matter? Much as some girls make out it does (and that we're all comparing you behind your backs on girls' nights out): not really. The myth has come about partly because of all the scrutiny women feel their own bodies to be under. Pathetically, it's a kind of revenge. Revenge for something largely imagined by women. Anyone who's been around a bit knows that it's other women and the advertising industry that make us paranoid about our body shape, not you. You're easily pleased creatures who, when you get a girl naked, don't think, 'Blimey, look at her cellulite' or 'I wish those breasts were bigger,' but rather 'Great – a naked female body.'

On the subject of penises, I've only ever been witness to conversations between girls about intimidatingly large ones and what to do when faced with one. What it can do for a man is give him the type of confidence that attracts women.

Everyone attaches an obvious kind of base, cartoon virility to the guy who's hung like a donkey – as they do to girls with big boobs – but it's honestly not a genuine concern. Bear the following in mind if you're worried about penis size:

- Seduce her mind – Zzzzzz. It's probably not what you want to hear, but it's a lot easier to start the foreplay in the bar with your razor-sharp, not-at-all-numbed-by-alcohol wit, than it is in bed with your under-pressure member and the lights down low and expectations high. If she's on her way to being ready before you're even in the taxi, she won't be thinking about the size of your thing. She'll be thinking what a great time she's having.

- It's not the mass, it's the motion. You'll have heard this said before by women, and by all means ignore it and stay paranoid, but in all honesty we're not selfless enough to make it up – it's true. If you focus on her and leave her satisfied but panting for more, she won't even remember the size of your equipment – she'll just want you to get it out again at the earliest opportunity.

- We're not as obsessed by your penis as you are – sorry, this is another fact of life. You've been fiddling with it since you were in your cot. We started taking a vague interest more than a decade later – but even then only for as long as we were in bed with you.

- The average penis size is 5.5 inches when erect. If yours is longer, bully for you. If it's shorter, so what? As long as you've got a half-decent cunnilingus technique, you'll hear no complaints from us.

- If anything, it's girth and not length that counts. If you must quantify, let it be your old boy's girth. Put in scientific terms, the nerves inside us women can feel its width, but the average vagina is only 4 inches deep, so length means practically nothing to us. If you've got a big one we can ingeniously accommodate you if you're slow, careful and gentle, but if you drive it all the way home too fast, you're in danger of just jabbing at our cervix and no one likes that. Makes the eyes water just to think about it.

WHAT TO DO IF IT'S HER 'TIME OF THE MONTH'

I know: it's every bloke's worst nightmare. You've put in all that effort and expertise, only to find when you get her home that the painters and decorators are in – and they're not sprucing up your shag pad to make this a sure-fire thing for you. They're putting the kibosh on the fun instead ... or are they? My advice would be: don't panic. Though she might be flying the Japanese flag, it doesn't necessarily mean the finish flag for the night's recreation.

For a start, some girls are hugely horny when they've got their period. She may be more up for it than at any other time in her cycle. So make the most of it: follow her lead. Other girls might be a bit more reticent. The best thing to do in that instance is to show her that you're completely cool with it, which will put her at her ease. Every girl feels differently about which sexual antics she's happy with at this time – but she does know what she's up for. The unknown factor is you. Prove that you're willing to go as far as she is and she'll happily jump into bed with you for whatever delights await.

Remember: penetration isn't the be-all and end-all. Though some girls will merrily indulge in this anyway, if she doesn't want to do it on this occasion, it doesn't mean you can't still have a hell of a lot of fun. So don't shoot yourself in the foot by dismissing her the moment she mentions the menstrual thing, be understanding and attentive. Keep on finding her mind-blowingly beautiful ... and at the very least your chances of snagging a blow job are still sky-high.

Key Erogenous Zones:
A Refresher Course

No matter how well you know or don't know your conquest, it's always worth concentrating on her pleasure. This is not just because she's more likely to reciprocate (girls are polite: if you give her something, she'll be keen to return the favour). It's not that she'll be more willing to go for it if she's out of her mind with lust; or because the wetter she is, the better the shag. It's not even because if she's happy, you're more likely to get laid – though this is, of course, a rather important consideration. Instead, it's your review rating that you've got to bear in mind. Whether or not this shag will lead to anything long-term is unclear. The word-of-mouth credit for you afterwards could well come in handy next weekend. Make her happy, she'll tell the world and you'll start building a reputation that'll have girls lining up to become your lover. And you can't argue with that.

One word of warning: being *too* conscientious a lover or getting too hung up on erogenous zones ruins things for everyone. But that's not to say you shouldn't try to find them – in fact, I'd recommend it. Erogenous zones vary – and move – according to the girl, her mood, who she's with, where in her menstrual cycle she is and what's gone before. So you can have lots of fun searching for those special places that drive her wild. On a good night, the whole body feels like an erogenous zone. Having said that, there's never any harm in dropping by to see old friends:

Lips and Mouth
Ridiculously sensitive, these, so don't just kiss them, nibble them lightly, catching one then the other in your lips; lick them a little – just teasingly. Touch them. Toy

with them with any part of your body you can think of. Don't go straight into a clumsy, high-school French kiss, but when your tongue does begin exploring inside, and as the intensity increases, gently touch the roof of her mouth with your tongue. Trust me.

Face

Despite Hollywood movies to the contrary, this is a surprisingly under-explored zone. Perhaps it takes a special degree of courage to look into someone's eyes and touch their face that other parts don't demand. At the very least, while you're kissing her try exploring the texture of the skin on her cheek with your fingertips – she'll love it.

Breasts

You can do any number of things to these. Tweaking them and sucking them is just the beginning. As you start, go gently: brush the undersides of them, and the sides where they hang over her ribs if she's lying on her back. Tease, tease, tease. Save the serious grabbing and nipping until she's really aroused – and even then go carefully: neither of you wants a reality check when you're in the throes of passion. Ouch.

Abdomen

During foreplay I think little teasing brushes with the backs of the fingertips work wonders here. Men and women both love the lightest of flicking sweeps with a fingernail up or down, just below and parallel to the bottom rib.

Bum

Speaking as a girl, it's great to have your hips or your bum cheeks grabbed by your lover when he's inside you. Before then, though, don't forget this highly sensitive part of her body. Run your hands down her back and finish by cupping her buttocks firmly, squeezing them with your whole hand. She'll feel like she's irresistible to you. Bottom fondling should be reserved for those you've at least spoken to – not to be applied to strangers in bars.

Clitoris

You think you know where this is – after all, you've been around a bit – but make absolutely sure. Have a good look with the light on. Take a torch down if she'll let you. Different girls' clitorises are in different places. That's before we've even begun on the range of its responses – both between different women and in the same one. As with the breasts, go easy and gentle to start with. She'll let you know when she wants the pressure increased. If you make her sore: instant final curtain for the night's entertainment.

Vagina

Does it need saying? Don't just make a beeline for this, however much The Captain orders it. He can wait. Start to combine the attention you're paying to the clitoris with little bits of attention to her vagina with your mouth or fingers. Seek out her G spot, perhaps, with a finger crooked on to the front of her vaginal wall about an inch or two up, but do it when she's already aroused. If you can't find it, don't die trying. Hold off from getting inside her until she's drenched for you. It'll be all the more heavenly when you finally slip inside, I promise.

Great Sex Myths

It's great to have a bit of variety, but don't believe the hype surrounding these sex myths:

- Doing it in front of the fire. Two sets of two words: carpet burns; scorched flesh.
- Doing it in water. Not only tricky logistically, but dangerous. The water washes away natural lubrication and can cause her internal damage. Plus condoms don't work as well, being prone to slipping off.
- Standing up. What are the chances of you being the same height/strong enough to hold her on to you?
- Threesomes. You'll want it with two girls; she'll want it with two men; the one who doesn't get their way will end up feeling left out.
- Girl-on-girl action. A famous rapper once said that any woman was only a couple of Sea Breezes away from a threesome. He should have added 'with a famous rapper'. While it's true that women can be the sexually ravenous creatures of your dreams, put simply, wanting to do it with a woman must involve wanting ladies' bits. Would you do the same for her?
- Anal sex is only fun for a man. Women do like it too. But not all. And go easy: lots of licking, gentle probing and front-bottom action first. You want it? You're going to have to work for it.
- Sex in public. Not even making mention of the potential discomfort (think Cally and those tree branches at the wedding, page 76), sex in public can be cold, awkward, unsexy and downright illegal. Beware security cameras. Everyone has seen those CCTV programmes where lone security guards get their kicks over long dark nights by watching couples having sex in lifts. The fact is, there's always an audience to consider:

Case Study: Sam

Sam was working in a bar one night, when she ended up having sex with a guy on the pool table after hours. Unfortunately, she'd forgotten that the bar had cameras trained on the table so it didn't get damaged. She and her lover were putting on a damn good show for the large band of stragglers left in the top bar.

A note on doing it doggy style: watch this. Some girls don't like it and even the most enthusiastic are going to raise an eyebrow or two if it's all you want to do – not that you'll see that because you can't see her face (and you're presumably too busy imagining someone else in her place). Give each position a proper chance, but don't get stuck in a rut sexually. Throw in the doggy, but get a good mix of other positions too.

Tantric Sex

A word of warning: if you fancy yourself as a bit of a Mr Tantric Loverman, make sure there's more in it for your partner than there was for my friend Jane. Her new lover was clearly something of a free spirit and told her he was into tantric sex. 'Great,' she thought, as images of Sting and prolonged periods of foreplay formed themselves in her mind.

The big night arrived: their first time together. It was never to be a particularly spontaneous, escapist experience for her ... because she was peeking throughout, wondering what this tantric business was all about. Actually, Mr Tantric Loverman proved a rather selfish lover – the only difference between him and her others being what happened to him at the point of climax. His eyes rolled upwards into his head, so that it looked like she was being seen to by a kind of scary orgasmic demon.

Pulling Your Partner

Couples are terrible for getting into habits sexually. But the most arousing thing is that you're still being aroused by each other. Keep trying new things, even if it's just shaking up when you have sex and where. Buy a bottle of wine or two, rent a DVD she'd find erotic – ask her if you're not sure, don't guess – and let the film open out into a conversation about fantasies. She may have been hankering after something filthy that you never knew about all this time. Remember, she's still sexual, however long you've been together and even if she doesn't always reveal it to you. Coax it out of her.

Case Study: Fiona

Fiona is a charismatic fifty-something woman who has been married for years and has three children of college age. Once, when she was bemoaning the fact that all her friends seem to get divorced once their children leave school, I asked her the secret of her and her husband Rod's success. Her reply was two words long: 'Dirty weekends.' They'd always had at least one a month and she was convinced it had kept them together.

Banned in Bed

Do any of the following – before or after the main event – and the drought which prompted you to read this book is destined to begin all over again. You have been warned.

- Saying, 'How about a game of Name the Stain?'
- Saying, 'Does your sister want to join us?' (That'll be a 'No'.)
- Engaging her in a discussion about your top ten lads'-mag pin-up girls ...
- ... Or your top ten modes of masturbation.
- ... Or your top ten imagined scenarios for masturbation.
- Revealing your fewest number of strokes-to-orgasm when masturbating.
- Crying on her shoulder, telling her your problems and asking for advice on women (you might scoff now, but wait until you've drunk eight pints, got a bit of affection from a stranger and find yourself feeling oddly lonely in the wee small hours).
- Sharing anecdotes which showcase your prowess with other girls. She doesn't want to feel like she's just another notch on your bedpost, even if she is.
- Saying, 'You're on your period? I think I'll go back to the bar then.'

Most important of all:

- *Don't say the wrong name.* If you forget her name, ask her if she has a nickname (you can then use that instead). If you're really desperate, give her a nickname of your own (not 'Thingy'). If she's foreign, ask her to remind you how to pronounce her name and hope she doesn't say, 'Er, Jane.' If ever in doubt, *never* guess.

So ... you've done it. Ding dong. Well done. Didn't I say you could? Didn't you know you could? The old boy's back in business, and all is right with the world.

You're probably ready for a nap right now. But here's a quick checklist, to ensure you both go away satisfied.

Sex: Checklist

Have you:

1. Snogged her face off?

2. Seduced her body?

3. Given her pleasure? (Did she moan like a good 'un? Did she writhe uncontrollably on your sheets? Did she need a moment to catch her breath? If yes to all three, well done that man.)

4. Slapped on a condom? (Safety first.)

5. Done the deed?

6. Enjoyed the orgasm to end all orgasms?

Well, there you have it: this book did get you laid. Sleep tight. She'll be waiting for you in the morning, I'm sure.

Appendix:
After the Event

Post-Coital Etiquette
Immediately after the action:

- Stay awake – if you want to be in with a shout of a second shag.
- If you decide to fix yourself an elaborate sandwich – offer her one too. If you're up to it, perhaps throw in some of the aphrodisiacs mentioned on page 116 – but not all at once.
- If you fancy a post-coital cigarette, check she's cool with it, then offer her one too.
- Hold off from texting your mates to tell them of your conquest until after she's gone.
- Ditto having a very long shower and scrubbing yourself clean. Suggest she uses the bathroom first and try to remember to smile and say, 'Good morning' when you wake up.
- Think back and deduce whether or not she had an orgasm. If the answer's 'no', resolve to do better next time.

How to Be a Gentleman
When you wake up in the morning, don't:

- Scratch your privates.
- Admire your Morning Glory – or expect her to.

- Proffer your MG – saying, 'I suppose a blow job's out of the question?'
- Slam the loo lid and seat – up and then down.
- Piss loudly and with 'aaaah, uuurgh' noises – and with spillage.
- Fart with such force that if she wasn't awake already, she sure as hell is now ... and then wonder why she doesn't want sex in the morning. We all have different ways of celebrating the arrival of a new day. Listening to you letting off isn't necessarily hers.
- Neglect to flush the toilet – whatever the damage.
- Leave marks on the side of the toilet bowl – it's grimmer than grim. You may as well tell her straight out that you see toilet cleaning as her territory.

Wily Coyote's Tips for Extricating Yourself

Everybody's heard the term 'coyote ugly', used when a person wakes up and, upon seeing what their conquest of the previous night looks like, decides they would be willing to gnaw their own arm off – like a coyote in a trap does – in order to get away.

Though you might feel like running for the hills, screaming at the top of your voice, think again. You've got to keep your wits about you. Do you want her to wake up? Shouting the house down in horror will merely rouse this sleeping 'beauty'. Having said that, I wouldn't recommend just leaving, even though every cell in your body is crying out for you to do just that. If you really can't bear to say a mumbled 'Hello' to her, at least leave a note thanking her for a great night. Manners are important.

Once she's woken, you're going to need a good get-out line to get yourself out of this situation, and out of having breakfast with Frankenstein's bride. A line that necessitates a sharp-harp exit, while discouraging future contact. Try one of the following (not all at once or she'll know it's overkill):

- 'Oh my God! I had a message from my boss last night. They're transferring me to Australia. I have to go pack.'
- 'I've just learned my parents are getting a divorce. This has completely shattered my belief in meaningful relationships.'
- 'I'd love to stay for breakfast, but I have this recurring stomach complaint and I can feel it coming on now. My bottom is going to explode any second. I hate this. It happens every time I've been with a girl.'
- 'My ex just called – to propose. I've realized she's The One. Do excuse me, I've a wedding to organize.'

Sometimes, if you're lucky, the dawning realization of the hugeness of your error occurs even before there has been any action. Perhaps it's still the night before, and your potential pull is already showing signs of being a bit of a psycho. How to escape?

- Lie – anything will do, but this is a safe bet: 'I'm sorry, my flatmate's just texted me; he's got a job interview in the morning and he's locked out. I'll have to go and let him in. Here's my (no longer functioning) email.'
- Out-psycho them – summon tears over a woman who you *know* loves you, even though she's rejected the several poems and flowers that you send her every week. Or make casual mention of the depraved sexual practices which you expect of a woman as a matter of course.

- Act naturally – tell her you've had a lovely evening, it's been nice meeting her, but you really should be going home now. If she wants to see you a second time, feign mild surprise and palm her off with, 'I'm sure we'll run into each other again.' Or give her that non-functioning email address.

Lived to Shag Another Day?

Coyote-ugly moments aside, all's gone well, it's the next morning and you've got laid. Result! You da man. But does she still think so?

Sure Signs This is the Last You'll See of Her

- Her saying, 'I'll call you.'
- Her scouring your flat for possible items left behind.
- Her leaving naked.
- Her smiling weakly and saying, 'See you soon!' hurriedly over her shoulder as she scrambles out. Perversely, 'soon' in this context means 'not for ages/never'; 'see you later' means soon, possibly later that day.

But You Know You're In if ...

- She sticks around/wants you to.
- She wants more sex.
- She makes you coffee.
- Breakfast rolls into lunch, which rolls into a takeaway in front of a DVD, then marriage, kids, etc.
- She's tidying your flat and making you breakfast.
- She's texting friends excitedly.
- She's smiling.

Finally, if the two of you show signs of being capable of seducing each other indefinitely, discard all the rules, get hold of each other ... and never let go.

All Michael O'Mara titles are available by post from:

Bookpost, PO Box 29, Douglas, Isle of Man, IM99 1BQ
Credit cards accepted
Telephone: 01624 677237 Fax: 01624 670923
Email: bookshop@enterprise.net
Internet: www.bookpost.co.uk
Free postage and packing in the UK

Other titles from Michael O'Mara Books:

The Hangover Companion: A Guide to the Morning After

It was only meant to be a quick couple of drinks, but it turned into a bit of a session. You woke up in the morning and the evil drinkie gorilla had broken into your room while you were unconscious, scattered your clothes across the floor, stolen all your money, stuck a traffic cone on your head and then crapped in your mouth. As you surf the peaks and troughs of the morning hangover, seek solace, even a cure, in the pages of *The Hangover Companion*. Includes:

- Hangover cures
- The truth about booze
- Quips and quotes from people who should know better
- Strange but true drinking stories

You'll be ready to face your next drink before you can say, 'Mine's a mineral water.'

£4.99
ISBN (10 digit): 1-84317-213-5
ISBN (13 digit): 978-1-84317-213-0

Man Skills: A Training Manual for Men

Nick Harper

The problem with men these days is that they know bugger all about the really important skills in life. They may be able to exfoliate and download and all that modern nonsense but, faced with a dripping tap or a fish that needs gutting, most men will have to look it up in a book, or phone their dads.

Somewhere along the line, a vital communication link between most fathers and sons has short-circuited. All the marvellous skills the older generation mastered, all the wisdom of a lifetime spent fixing, catching and bludgeoning stuff to death, have somehow failed to transfer to the modern man.

Indeed, Nick Harper reached the age of thirty-two before realizing he didn't even know the basics, so he scratched his head for a while before deciding to learn them. Not all of them, of course, that would be impossible, but the essentials – like how to wire a plug, win at arm-wrestling, and undo a lady's bra with one hand; and how to choose a suit, bleed a radiator, and dance without looking like a hapless moron.

It took some time but here, at long last, is *Man Skills* – the humble guide to being just a bit less crap.

£9.99
ISBN (10 digit): 1-84317-230-5
ISBN (13 digit): 978-1-84317-230-7

Tricks to Freak Out Your Friends

Pete Firman
Foreword by Derren Brown

How many times have you wanted to bring a fly back to life with just the power of your mind? Stop your own pulse? Stick a skewer through your tongue? Lots? Then you *need* this book.

Tricks to Freak Out Your Friends is chock-a-block full of sick, rude and downright scary feats of offbeat magic. This isn't another of those run-of-the-mill conjuring collections featuring rabbits and hats; this, my friends, is an *adult* magic book. TV's coolest 'street' magician Pete Firman presents tricks to perform in the pub, at home, in restaurants and out and about. Whether it's popping your eyeball with a fork, cutting off your thumb or levitating, these tricks are guaranteed to make people think you've sold your mother to Lucifer.

Go on, give your mates a magical kick in the nuts!

Pete Firman combines sorcerer, comedian, TV star and all-round entertainment guy in one astonishing package. He is a uniquely gifted magician, mischievously injecting the genre with his offbeat humour and dazzling array of skills. He has recently starred in Channel 4's *Dirty Tricks*, Five's *Monkey Magic* and Sky One's *The Secret World of Magic*, and can often be seen performing in a comedy club near you.

£9.99
ISBN (10 digit): 1-84317-207-0
ISBN (13 digit): 978-1-84317-207-9

Crap Teams

Geoff Tibballs

No longer relegated to oblivion, the rubbish runs and shameful seasons of the world's worst football teams are championed in *Crap Teams*. Even the best clubs have the odd off-day and, as this book proves, having a full-to-bursting trophy cabinet, or even a tabloid darling on the ball, is just no guarantee of sporting success. From globally popular Man United to the record-breaking Gunners, each and every tip-top team has had seasons and shoot-outs they'd rather forget. Unfortunately for them, *Crap Teams* provided the searing post-match analysis of their flings with failure, laying bare the facts, the stats and the shame of each footballing fiasco.

Packed with illustrations and trivia from both on and off the pitch, and with side-splitting segments on the international tournaments, *Crap Teams* recalls those embarrassing years that the nation's favourite teams would rather forget: when game after game went to Underdog United, FA Cup certainties were converted to giant-slaying massacres, and million-pound strikers found scoring in a brothel beyond them. Spanning nearly forty years of glorious incompetence, *Crap Teams* is the indispensable guide to the heartache, hilarity and humiliation of the UK's most useless seasonal squads. Read it and weep.

£9.99
ISBN (10 digit): 1-84317-111-2
ISBN (13 digit): 978-1-84317-111-9